BRAVE & *Beautiful*

GOD'S PEARL GIRL

FIONA MELLETT

Scripture quotations noted NIV are from The Holy Bible, New International Version NIV. Copyright 1973, 1978, 1984, 2011 by Biblica, Inc. Used by permission. All rights reserved worldwide.

Library of Congress Catalog Number
ISBN 978-0-9960596-0-2

Dedication

I dedicate this book to my brave and beautiful children Colin, Aiden, Celia Kate, Gracie, and Sean.

I pray that your God-stories will be even greater than mine, that your spirits carry a double portion of what Daddy and I have and that you know God's heart and hear his voice louder than anything else in this world including your own. Each one of you has seeds of greatness on the inside. Putting Jesus first will allow those seeds to grow and flourish. You are mighty oaks of righteousness in the making and I love you with all my heart!

BRAVE & BEAUTIFUL

Acknowledgments

Thank you Lord Jesus. I bless you for giving me the strength and perseverance to accomplish this work. Your grace has sustained me, empowered me and moved me forward. I praise you for these God stories. It is my greatest joy to follow you.

Thank you Michael Mellett, my extraordinarily awesome, handsome and loving husband. This would never have been possible without your vision, leadership and encouragement. I would have waited another decade for you. You are worth far more than any sacrifice I've ever had to make. Every day with you is a gift. I love you Mush!

Thank you my precious children, Colin, Aiden, Celia Kate, Gracie and Sean, for praying big, bold and powerful prayers for Mommy. You are such a joy and inspiration to my life!

Dad and Mom Delamere, how could I ever thank you enough for all the faith you have poured into my life. Your prayers have transformed me, prepared me and preserved me. Thank you for being an example of believing God in the midst of adversity, seeking him with all your hearts and being filled by him daily. You never tire of speaking life, encouraging others and looking for Kingdom opportunities. I'm proud to be your daughter.

Mom Mellett, my mighty praying mother-in-love, I bless God for making us family. Thank you for carrying me through with your encouragement and prayers! Only heaven will tell all that you've been up to on my behalf. Thank you for praying in my basherter! Love never fails!

Thank you Lakewood Church Choir for all your encouragement and open hearts. I love preaching to the choir! You are an awesome group of people, truly the salt of the earth and I am privileged to be in ministry with you. Thank you for encouraging me to "write the book"!

Thank you Rich Catapano, Clayton and Marlene Glickert, Don Foster, Jim and Mary DeGolyer, AnnMarie and Pat Mercadante, Richard and Blanca Mojica, Marco and Carla Barrientos, Danilo and Gloriana Montero, George and Sylvia Pfahl, Mrs. Morgan, Joel and Victoria Osteen, Darlene Zschech and Mrs. Dodie Osteen. Your godly example, spiritual covering and guidance have helped mold my life and faith.

Thank you Simonton Community Church and all your Pearl Girls. Your encouragement and support are priceless!

Lisa Moscarelli and Moscarelli Media, your intercession, generosity, master media and faithful encouragement carried me full term... You are a Godsend!

Amy Oglesby and Gretchen Simmen thank you for letting me crash at your homes to write!

Pamela Faye Johnson! I bless God for you! You are an awesome editor, intercessor and friend!

Special thanks to Gabriela Caicedo, Sera and Darryn Johnson, Steve and Tammy Crawford, Craig and Corinne Dunn, Paul and Chermaine, Shaw and Marcus and Cindy Ratcliff.

Thank you Linda Bourdeaux at TheDesignDesk.com for your amazing graphics inside and out. Thank you Eric Forsythe at ForsythePhotography.com for capturing a moment of truth on film and adding your wisdom and fine support.

To all my family and friends, it is such a joy to be on this journey together! The best is yet to come!

Endorsements

Brave & Beautiful is a powerful expression of God's heart for women. God is for her in every season of the soul. Fiona's God-stories will ignite fresh faith, freedom and a longing to know the One who calls you Brave and Beautiful. These pearls of truth are for every girl on the planet!
—Darlene Zschech

Today, there are fantasy princesses and redheaded heroines capturing the imagination of many young girls. But no fictional tale will ever be as moving as a real life, heart-inspiring story. This is Fiona's story, full of faith and boldness, shining and challenging us to the core. You will not be disappointed as you read of her fearless trust in God, and her willingness to wait for His best for her. She is the real deal!
—Marco and Carla Barrientos

Knowing Fiona personally, I can attest that she is indeed brave and beautiful. To me, she is the perfect person to write a book that expresses God's heart for His daughters, or as she refers to us, His "Pearl Girls". If you long to see yourself the way your Creator sees you, and live the life He planned before you were formed, *Brave & Beautiful* is the book for you.
—Mandisa

Brave & Beautiful is the best description of Fiona's faith. In full color and vibrancy she shares the strength of her Irish-American family; takes you on her world travels and unfolds a cinematic love story that culminates in New York. But much more than this, she will take you by the hand for an undeniable encounter with the reality of God. It's inevitable to sit and listen to Fiona without coming away changed. Her devotion, passion and love for God and life are contagious. As you read, prepare to begin your own adventure of faith, a faith that is brave and beautiful!
—Danilo and Gloriana Montero

Brave & Beautiful is an inspired reminder to us all that we are made in the image of God, and that each of us was designed by Him to succeed, to flourish and to make our own unique contribution to the world. My friend Fiona Mellett truly is a brave and beautiful woman. I believe this book will encourage you to see yourself in a new way and to become all God created you to be.
—Victoria Osteen, *New York Times* bestselling author and Co-Pastor, Lakewood Church in Houston, Texas.

Brave & Beautiful

Once upon a time not so long ago
There was a little girl with red curls, freckles on her nose
She said, "Lord I'm willing whatever you want to do.
I'll follow you"
And in her heart she heard Him say

I call you Brave and Beautiful. You are my treasure
You are my pearl. Crown of creation
With strength and bold determination

Lord I believe, in you I can be ... Brave and Beautiful

She grew up, had a family of her own. She loves her home
And she gives it all she's got
But she still needs to hear those tender words.
They carry her
And in her heart she hears Him say

I call you Brave and Beautiful
You are my treasure
You are my pearl
Crown of creation
With strength and bold determination

Lord I believe, in you I can be ... Brave and Beautiful

Every little girl needs to hear these words
Every woman needs to know her worth
Every season of a woman's soul
Created to fulfill her destiny she was made to leave a legacy
That's the reason why she needs to know

He calls you Brave and Beautiful
You are his treasure. You are his pearl
Crown of creation, With strength and bold determination
Will you believe
In Him you can be
Brave & Beautiful

"My son [and daughter], if you accept my words
And store up my commands within you,
Turning your ear to wisdom and
applying your heart to understanding,
And if you call out for insight
and cry aloud for understanding,
And if you look for it as for silver
and search for it as for hidden treasure,
Then you will understand the fear of the Lord
And find the knowledge of God.

For the Lord gives wisdom and from his mouth
come knowledge and understanding.
He holds victory in store for the upright,
He is a shield to those whose walk is blameless,
For He guards the course of the just
and protects the way of His faithful ones.
Then you will know what is right and just and fair
– every good path.

For wisdom will enter your heart,
and knowledge will be pleasant to your soul.
Discretion will protect you and understanding
will guard you."
—Proverbs 2:1-11

Forward By Michael Mellett

We sat face to face in the airport that day. The setting sun was at my back and casting a light on Fiona's face. At that moment, neither of us knew what was ahead. We were merely friends. As I looked at her smile, illuminated by the sun, I noticed how beautifully iridescent her teeth were. Caught slightly off guard, I remarked, "Your teeth are so pearlescent." She thanked me for the compliment and life moved on. Somehow, it was a strange glimpse into the future- almost as if my spirit knew something long before my mind caught up. Until this point, we had always managed to avoid the suggestions of dating made by family members (mainly, my sister-in-law, Debbie) when we would see each other during holiday visits at my brother's home in New York. Even then, we would sing duets together and play songs we had written. It was that very thing that had brought us back into contact. Fiona was visiting me to begin working on a recording project that I was to produce for her. Now, here we were awaiting her return flight to New York, with the sunlight illuminating something I had not noticed until then.

Two years later, when Fiona moved to Nashville, those "illuminating moments" began to happen with greater frequency. What we had ruled out as a possibility because we were "too alike", culturally, musically, as well as a host of other preconceived notions, soon began to lose their grip; and we found ourselves growing in love. It was an orchestrated, moment-by-moment, momentum-gaining, slow building, romance that God alone could set into motion. This God-adventure was almost undetected as it culminated into the most miraculous display of weaving one life into another until we were both left speechless at the perfection of His will and timing. This love, birthed in God's heart, is one that I would have waited an eternity for. Now, almost 15 years later, we are constantly amazed at how deep the love runs between us and at how it continues to grow. Our love is a love nurtured in the fertile soil of God's love for us.

Fiona's fresh perspective on this journey will ignite a desire for the same kind of relationship she has with God. As the pages of this book will show, the truest love story is the one God has written into every page of his Word, the Bible. These stories will remind you that the greatest adventure awaits those who will run headlong into His arms and say, "I trust you!" He is waiting to unravel the mysteries of His Kingdom to those willing to embrace His calling for their lives. I am privileged to call this woman my wife and to have witnessed firsthand many of the stories she tells. Fiona continues to be one of my greatest heroes of the faith because that is truly how she lives every day! Be inspired as you read this account of a life of faith, lessons learned, and love revealed!

Contents

Preface

I started writing this book over 10 years ago. I was going to call it *The Great Wait*, as waiting upon God for my husband became a season of life I will treasure forever. It was truly Great! I blossomed in the midst of waiting and then realized I was no longer waiting for a man to complete me but one who would compliment me as I was already complete in Christ. Yes, I was lonely at times and longed to be a double, rather than a single; but trusting God and handing him the reins of my life proved to be the greatest choice I would make. Life is much more fun when you are following God's lead. There are no regrets and the doors he opens are greater than anything you could have pulled off on your own!

In the Spanish language to *wait* (esperar) is the same word used for *hope* (esperanza). And when a woman is expecting a baby, they use the word *esperando,* which is *waiting, hoping and expecting* all in one. Basically to wait is to hope and to expect. I think that's true in life. If you are willing to wait on God for the best in any given situation in life you are hoping and expecting. Hope is what keeps faith alive. I had to wait until I was 30 years old to get married. I had to wait for God to open the right ministry opportunities. I had to wait for children and so many other dreams in my heart. But most importantly, I had to learn to wait on God to truly hear him; hoping and expecting all along the way.

The question I am asked most frequently is "How *do* you hear God?" I have to say the first step is learning to stop and listen. That takes *waiting*. God is never in a hurry. Have you noticed?

Ten years ago I wrote over 100 pages to tell you these stories and then God said to leave it alone. I would not pick it back up again until it was absolutely God. As my family is my first priority, there was too much at stake. A year ago I was so surprised to hear God say it was time. I knew I would have the grace to get it done because it was God who was moving me forward. He wouldn't lead me to do something I wouldn't have the strength for. In the midst of a busy family of seven, pastoring on staff at the largest church in America and leading worship, God made it work! And His timing is impeccable!

The title *Brave & Beautiful* came as a refreshing surprise to me. Even the words *God's Pearl Girl* were truly like a gift to me after walking through different seasons of the soul. He gave me these words. I didn't choose them for myself. As you read, you will discover how my life's journey brought me to a place where I could identify with them. It was a *God-work* for sure!

My deepest desire is that you too will identify with these words. You were made by the world's greatest Designer, complete with a master plan to have a life full of power, love, and promise. You were created to know and experience your full worth, full potential, and full freedom. My prayer is that your heart will be encouraged no matter what season of the soul you are in. Today is your day. Your pearls are waiting!!

ONE

The Red Zone and Redheads

"For God has not given us a spirit of fear but of
power and love and a sound mind."
—II Timothy 1:7

It was 6am. The crisp Andes mountain air blew cool
across my face as I stepped onto the sidewalk. My adrenaline began to rush. I waved down the taxi that would take
me to the Quito International Airport. I was in Ecuador,
South America on my way to the neighboring country of
Colombia. It was an unusual trip. I was headed for a "red
zone," guerilla territory. I had heard about these dangerous
areas of the world where people could be kidnapped ran-
domly and ransomed for high sums of money. Some are
persecuted for their faith, others are taken advantage of because of their wealth. It was a risk for anyone who lived in
the area. The fact that I was a tall, single, young, American
woman traveling alone really didn't help. I was obvious,
with or without my long, curly red locks!

Originally my mother was going to meet me there but
the State Department in the US had contacted her in New
York saying it wasn't safe and that she shouldn't go. I'll never forget our conversation.

"I can't go, Fiona, but if you have peace, you can. Daddy
and I will pray."

I was surprised by her words but couldn't deny the fact that if God said to go I should go, He would protect me. I trusted him implicitly. My parents had observed this pattern in my life for years by now. They trusted him the same way and knew I would hear clearly and obey. It's the "peace factor." Got peace? Green light, go! No peace? Red light, no go!

I prayed about it and to my surprise I had peace.

So, here I was heading to guerilla territory with a fresh sense of adventure, the thrill of obedience and a peace that just wouldn't quit. Destiny was calling. I had picked up! We were on our way, and I was just 22 years old.

I hadn't planned to go alone. As a matter of fact, I wasn't planning on doing anything alone. My idea was to get married at 21 to some major ministry guy, have my first baby at 23 and go to the nations...with him! But when I arrived at that beautiful age and he was nowhere in sight I had a choice. I would either sit around waiting or I would follow the call of God on my own life and one day connect with him along the way. I'm so glad I decided not to hang around waiting. It would have been a lot longer than I ever imagined; and, my life would have been extremely mundane compared to what transpired over the next few years.

Here I was, moving full steam ahead; with or without him! I would pour myself out, give my best, serve with my whole heart and grow into the woman God was molding me to be. I had passion, vision, and utter devotion to Jesus. There was nothing holding me back now. No strings attached. I could follow Jesus with total abandon. I had the freedom to take every opportunity afforded to me, walk through every door - big or small, and climb through every little window. It was Jesus and me! And it was awesome!

My first flight into Colombia brought me to the capital city of Bogota, a beautiful and modern metropolis. Everything moved in a rhythm. There was progress in the making amidst the rolling green hills and thick city air. In all my years of gathering Spanish-speaking friends I observed that anyone from Colombia carried a unique confidence and joy. They are sanguine at the core and love celebrating life in the moment. There's no reason to keep calm and quiet down. Life is to be lived and they are passionate about it.

When I boarded my second flight the plane was considerably smaller. It reminded me once again that I was leaving my international connection and going to a remote area. I would be disconnecting, leaving all that was familiar and headed for the unknown. I watched as the city faded into the greenery and I was off to follow the "green light"... *the go of peace.*

Upon my arrival, I was told that the return flights would be delayed and I would be held in that area for a few days more than expected. I knew I needed to get in and out. Respectfully, I told them I could stay for 72 hours at the most. I had responsibilities. They were surprised by my forthrightness and quickly worked to guarantee a return flight. It would make for a shorter stay but that was okay.

My mission was to visit a special family; to affirm them, encourage their faith, share testimonies, pray, and be a blessing. Our time was precious. I knew there was more to it than I could see but I was just being obedient to do my part and trusted that God would do his. Before leaving, I hosted a luncheon and shared a beautiful meal with the family and their friend who was going to take me to the airport. Even though it was a short visit I had great peace when it was time to leave. Obedience always leaves you feeling complete. God had been speaking to me during the whole trip, giving me understanding about certain aspects of life and broadening my awareness. I was grateful.

Upon arriving at the airport, I was told that there was a delay and that the plane coming in would not arrive in time to make my connecting flight in the capital city of Bogota. This was the only plane leaving for the next four days. It was the only way I would be able to make the international flight. I started to pray, clinging to the peace that got me there.

Looking around I noticed a woman smiling at me. "Misionera?" she asked. (Missionary?) I returned the smile and confirmed with a nod. She kept smiling inquisitively so I explained my situation. Seeing my concern she agreed to pray as well. Suddenly, I noticed that the woman who drove me to the airport was walking up to the control tower where they directed the planes. It was a small airport with just about 30 people who all seemed to be waiting for the same plane. I knew this woman was a friend of the family but I didn't know she had any particular authority in the town. Most women in Latin culture don't carry this type of power. She motioned for me to come up to where they were discussing my situation. I climbed the stairs and noticed that she was speaking quite forcefully to the men behind the control panel. I explained that my mother and sister would arrive the next day in Quito and I had to be there to receive them. It was obvious this woman had a certain pull in the community. As soon as the plane arrived they were hurrying the passengers off and hurrying the new ones on. By this time they began treating me like a celebrity. I was taking pictures with the family while all the others were being rushed up the stairs. Then they insisted that I sit in first class. Now this was getting comical!

As we were about to land in Bogota, I remember the flight attendant asking if I was ready. I thought, "Sure, as long as you don't ask me to jump!" We hadn't even touched the ground yet! When we hit the tarmac she had me stand by the door. "How cool," I thought. The moment the plane stopped they opened the door while the attendant below was still rolling the steps up to the side of the plane. He yelled, "Es la Senorita Delamere?" (Is this Ms. Delamere?) We all yelled back, "Si!" I noticed a nice shuttle bus waiting by the steps. Yep, it was for me! I ran down with my bags and climbed in. There waiting for me was a representative from immigration ready to do my paperwork. I had never seen this before. He was stamping and signing as we went. They quickly drove me over to my next flight and dropped me off at the aircraft stairs as if I were the queen. This was a trip and a half!

Entering the plane I noticed everyone was leaning into the aisle staring at me. The grand 747 was packed. That's when I thought I'd ask the flight attendant how long they had been waiting. "Forty-five minutes," he stated emphatically. I quickly sat down in the first row, first class seat. By this time I was in awe. "God! What are you doing? You are just amazing me. Who am I that you would treat me with such distinction?" It seemed like a movie.

As I pondered the day's events, I felt humbled by the grace and favor that was rumbling over my life. I felt privileged. It seemed as though God had taken a moment to honor me for giving him first place. I had said *yes* to the call - following, praying, listening, and waiting. He wanted me to know he noticed the whole thing. The awe turned into tears of joy. How dear, how precious, how powerful it is to walk with God. I laughed my way back to Quito reflecting on all the details. "Who on earth was that lady telling everyone what to do in the tower? I'm just glad God put her on my path."

Upon arrival I was still floating. I jumped into the first taxi and told the driver where I was headed. It was a huge yellow car that looked more like a big banana. The backseat was enormous. As we made our way out of the airport gate the driver informed me it would cost 7,000 sucres. I knew it only cost 2,500; and, I told him so. He responded very abruptly that it would be 7,000 sucres or he would drive me around town until the meter read 7,000.

Well! I had just witnessed the creator of the universe orchestrate a perfect path for my return. There was no stinkin' way I would let someone take advantage of me now. Yes, the fire was lit. He was messing with the wrong senorita. I pulled myself up from that big backseat and leaned right up by his ear. With a loud authoritative voice I stated in Spanish, "Do you know who my Father is??!!! DO YOU KNOW WHO MY FATHER IS???!! Are you trying to get in trouble? I can get you in trouble. Stop the car, this minute!" The man started to shake. He pulled the car over immediately. I jumped out and waited by the trunk. He could have just ditched me with no bag but He came around slowly and took my bag out of the trunk. I yelled, "Gracias! Por Nada!" (Thanks! For nothing!) He took off in a hurry. Simultaneously I flagged down another taxi, this time for 2,500 sucres. That's more like it!

There was no doubt that God himself took careful watch over my life that day. I had been treated with such respect and dignity by my Heavenly Father. He cared deeply about his daughter. With him at the helm of my life, I was a force to be reckoned with! Sure I was still a humble missionary, living on a mere pittance, with no earthly status or reputation, but it was God himself who affirmed me. It was God who arranged my every blessing. I was his princess, and a fiery redheaded one at that.

Pearl Power

I didn't always feel courageous. Actually it took quite a bit of time and some repeated opportunities to cultivate the character of a brave heart. It also took time to embrace my true beauty. I had to work out my insecurities, practice my freedom, and realize who I really was. I had to learn how to appreciate myself for who God made me to be and accept the gift of me, a work in progress. But more than all this, I needed Jesus. Receiving his love, trusting his heart and hearing his still small voice would be the greatest treasure found in a lifetime. Nothing else would make complete sense without him, including my heart.

Like pearls hidden in deep dark places along the ocean floor, I began to discover these precious truths. At times they came in small realizations and unexpected opportunities, and then others came in moments of brutal honesty in the midst of joy and even deep sorrow. The pearls were waiting for me.

What amazed me about these pearls was that even though they were precious and priceless they were mine to be had as early in life as I was willing to accept them. I didn't have to grow up and prove myself worthy or responsible enough to receive such an awesome gift. They were free and I was free to receive them no matter where I grew up, what country I lived in, how educated I was, how much money my family had or what season of the soul I was in. When things seemed to fall apart and I had to pull myself back up, the pearls were still there, as true as ever. I cherished them even more.

Small Town, Big God

Let me take you back to my roots where it all started. I grew up in Mahopac, New York, a small town just an hour north of New York City. I am the third of five redheads all of whom are blessed to call Patrick and Kathleen Delamere parents. Our neighborhood was filled with a plethora of children who thrived on adventure. Growing up in Mahopac gave us the freedom of exploration. There were miles and miles of hills, trails, and lakes, a golf course, a miniature airport, and even historic graveyards to be discovered. It was an amazing place to experience as a child. We had the pleasure of making trips to the city for big events like the Radio City Christmas Spectacular or a climb to the top of the Empire State Building but our greatest joy was sharing the great outdoors in everyday living. It was the best of both worlds!

My mom didn't have an ounce of fear in her bones. She and Dad would pray each morning; and, after school or chores were done we were free to roam the hills and dales as long as we got home when the firehouse whistle blew. Their prayers would prove to be the greatest asset of our childhood.

Winters in Mahopac were known for long treks up the frozen rock-walled streams to the big lake, Lake Mahopac. We would carry thermoses filled with hot chocolate and our ice skates flung over our shoulders until we reached the open expanse of thick ice and snow. We would hurry to get our skates on and then head out to discover what was new on the three islands. Other days we would go sledding and tobogganing on the golf course, make snow angels and snowmen, or dig enormous white tunnels through our driveway snow piles. There was a long winter break, youth retreats, Christmas and New Year's church celebrations, school-canceled snow days, sleepovers, big puzzles, and all kinds of delicious food. Mom sure does know how to cook!

Spring faithfully brought transformation.   Life burst above the surface once again. The trees filled up with lush greenery. The woods were now camouflaged. Dancing in the rain was a must -jumping in puddles too. I witnessed many Robin's nests being filled with baby birds and new life popping up all around. The array of flowers always seemed to come as a surprise. We would take a trip to Ireland each Easter to visit my mom's family. By the time we got back everything had started to bud. The cherry tree over-whelmed the front yard with blossoms as well as the crabapple tree in the back. It was miraculous.

Summers were meant for camping, bike rides, swim-ming, water skiing, backyard campfires, s'mores, fresh gar-den vegetables, roller skating, root beer floats, pizza parties, more sleepovers, monopoly, card games, and teen camp. There was also weeding, cleaning, and laundry; but, I like to focus on what brought the most joy. There was never a dull moment and if one tried to come upon us it didn't last very long. Our imaginations would take off and then so would our bikes.   We had the challenge each Saturday of how many times we could make it around the six-mile lake. This, of course, included stops at the pizzeria and the ice cream shop (Carvel!)

Fall was always welcomed after a long, hot New York summer. The days started cooling off and the nights called for hooded sweatshirts. The task of raking large quantities of leaves was always relieved by the sheer joy of jumping off tree limbs into enormous piles of these crunchy, multicol-ored autumn treasures. Life was about creating our own adventure.   There were forts to build, trails to blaze, animals to catch, and God to be revealed. It was awesome!

9

The Greatest People on the Planet

"Honor your father and your mother, so that you may live
long in the land the Lord your God is giving you."
Exodus 20:12

My mother grew up on a farm in the hills of Northern
Ireland. She was the youngest of nine children. At eighteen
years of age she decided to come to the States to help her
sister who was getting married. Her plan was to become a
nun and maybe, one day, work in an African mission. Those
plans all came to a halt one Sunday. That morning she had
placed her last ten dollars in the offering plate at church for
the guest missionary. It was all she had for food and transportation that week. In the evening she decided to go to a
church dance where she met my father. Dad was born in
The Bronx to Irish immigrants. He was the oldest of four, a
hard working young man, filled with vision and ready to
settle down. He asked for her name. When she responded
Flory (short for Florence) in her lilting Irish accent, he asked
if she had another name (Flory didn't quite cut it for him).
She then offered Kathleen, which was actually her first
name. That sounded more like what he wanted to call his
future bride and from that moment on she remained Kathleen. He then rang home to let his mother know they would
be having a guest for dinner, the woman he would marry.
That was before asking my mother, of course. Tuesday he
went out, bought a car and had it put in her name. He was
obviously making plans. Every day that week he picked her
up for dinner and on Friday he unofficially asked for her
hand in marriage! Oh the simplicity!

As a teenager, my father had some serious leg and back
injuries that led him to seek chiropractic care. At the time,
he was bedridden when a family member helped him into

the backseat of a station wagon and drove him to New Jersey to see the only chiropractor available in the region. After experiencing some remarkable results, Dad decided to pursue a career in chiropractic to help others. After completing his studies he began attending seminars. At one particular meeting he was encouraged to choose his words carefully and keep a tight rein on his tongue. He was taught that what he believed of himself and what he spoke was powerful. Every word carried weight. He began implementing this with his patients and in his personal life. He could see that speaking positively or negatively made an impact on his life. This helped him push past a lot of fear.

At the seminars the head chiropractor would tell the other doctors that "death and life are in the power of the tongue," words spoken right out of Proverbs. He explained that they could choose life and speak it. My father wanted to see people healed and wanted very much to be free from all the fear he grew up with; so, he got a hold of this principle. It was just the beginning of his journey to Jesus, his Savior and Healer. A couple of years later he met my beautiful mother.

After settling down and gaining their first addition to the family, my brother Kieran Patrick, they moved out of the city to a little town an hour north of Manhattan where his chiropractic practice thrived. Because of his lesson regarding words Dad always spoke about our family with the highest regard. He made us sound special and important. He knew he could bless our home or curse it. He taught us to respect our family name – not because we came from greatness but because it was "ours." It was the right thing to do. I'm sure it was quite a challenge at times knowing he came from a very difficult and poverty stricken background. Dad may not have always felt this way but he chose to speak it. He must have had to push past a mountain of insecurities every time he opened his mouth; yet, he did it and it made a difference.

When we were still babies my father began calling each one of us by royal names: Prince, Duke, Princess, Duchess, and Lady D. I was named "The Duchess" and I loved it. Still do. I identified with that word. One day I took a walk down to our local grocery store, Red Mills Market. There was a man on a ladder fixing a light. He looked down at me, smiled and said, "You must be your daddy's princess?" I smiled back and quickly corrected him saying, "Oh no, I'm the Duchess!" He roared laughing but I knew my place. I had identified myself with that word and even *princess* couldn't sway me, ha! It felt strong and secure. I was happy to be "The Duchess!"

The amazing thing was that, years later when I was almost a teenager, my father decided to delve into some family history. He encountered the most extraordinary information. My father's ancestors were actually kings and queens in the 12th century. They had come from France and brought the Franciscans with them. Basically they brought Christianity to Ireland. There was an abbey, a monastery, and a cemetery to prove it. We took the trip as a family and found it all!

This find was astounding, as my father had grown up in a very poor family with many challenges. Royalty was far from their vocabulary. Seeing what was written amazed us all. It affirmed our identity and confirmed what we had been speaking all along. Duchess indeed!

My parents honored their parents. They never spoke of them in a dishonoring tone even though I'm sure they didn't always agree. My father chose to forgive and honor his father in some very difficult circumstances. He never spoke ill of him. Never. I bless my father for choosing God's way. It is an amazing example. He surely has reaped some serious benefits from that promise. I learned this principle early on and it brought such blessing, freedom and even protection to my life. It's a core life truth that God upholds. No wonder honoring parents is one of the Ten Commandments.

Pearl Power

You have the power to choose to honor your parents, whether you agree with them or not and even when they are not "worthy" of your honor. This truth can protect and bless your life. And God will honor you for it. "Honor your father and mother – which is the first commandment with a promise - that it may go well with you and that you may enjoy long life on the earth" — Ephesians 6: 2

Jesus First

My parents made the decision to give God the reins of their lives the year I was born. They became passionate about following Jesus. It was not a tradition or a religious obligation but a joy to know God more deeply and receive freedom, healing, and truth. They believed wholeheartedly and began the journey of trusting Jesus as their Savior and Lord. We still had many challenges but there was room for God to work, heal, and inspire.

The greatest tool they got a hold of for parenting was prayer. Praying bold prayers, praying scripture, praying what they could not see as if it were already in place. They would ask God for help with everything and anything.

I remember seeing Mom on her knees early in the morning crying out to God for us children. She would be speaking the word. "As for these children they will grow in wisdom and stature and favor with God and man." "All my children will be taught by the Lord and great shall be their peace. In wisdom they will be established and tyranny will be far from them." "No weapon formed against them will prosper and every voice that rises up against them will be refuted." My mother was fierce when it came to prayer and worship. It made me feel secure and gave me a desire to do the same. My father filtered everything through the verse, "Death and life are in the power of the tongue." He knew that we would either build our future or tear it down with our words and he always made us accountable for what we spoke. It made me think twice before just saying whatever popped into my head. And there was plenty of popping.

As a child I believed and made my own decision to follow Jesus. I knew his love and had experienced his forgiveness even at five years of age. I knew I needed God and I wanted to make him proud. I had heard special speakers give testimonies about going through a radical experience when they gave their hearts to God. It was as if they had seen stars or heard fireworks going off in their hearts. I didn't have any fireworks or see any stars. So, I would make a trip to the altar quite frequently just to make sure. One Sunday I told my dad I just needed a date, a set time I could claim my decision for Christ. We prayed together and sealed the deal once and for all. Still no stars but I had a date and I was satisfied!

I had been baptized as an infant but when an itinerant evangelist came to our home and was baptizing people in our bathtub I wanted in, literally. It was a very large tub and I was now five. He returned when I was seven, this time baptizing people in the pool. I jumped in again. Years later I came to understand the purpose behind the command and longed to make a mature step of faith. So I was baptized at seventeen during the New Year's Eve service with one of my best friends, Jeannie. Isn't it good to know that God looks on the heart!

Seekers

One thing I have always admired about my folks is that they are seekers. They started seeking God and they never stopped. As a child they had a running Bible study and prayer group that met in our home regularly to worship God and seek him with their whole hearts. They would also take us each year to a Christian family conference. I looked forward to going each summer. It was exciting to grow in God. I loved being in His presence and worshipping him as a child.

The summer that I was seven we gathered with hundreds of families in Hershey, Pennsylvania at the annual conference. I remember being in a big room with a great number of children. We were all sitting with our legs crossed on the carpeted floor worshipping the Lord when the children's minister posed a question. He asked if we would like to receive a free gift from the Holy Spirit called our prayer language. He told us about the importance of having a prayer language and how we could use it when we didn't know how to pray. He also said it was like talking to God Spirit-to-spirit without interruptions and how God would strengthen our spirits and teach us how to pray. I thought that sounded great. So, I closed my eyes and with my childlike faith I asked God for my prayer language and just waited. I remember singing "Halleluiah" for a while. It was a few minutes later when I felt as if something was bubbling up in my belly (my spirit) and then these words came. They were not words I was familiar with in my mind but my spirit felt very comfortable; and, I felt especially close to God. I was so grateful because my mom and dad had their prayer language and I was blessed to share this gift. I knew it was special but I didn't realize how special at the time. It was much more powerful than I could have comprehended at the time. There was much to learn.

Pearl Power

Believing in Jesus as my Lord and Savior was the most important foundational truth I ever accepted. This was my own personal decision (not my parents) to believe God's word and accept it as truth. It was the greatest treasure I could have ever received. I really didn't have a clue how awesome it was at the time. I could only see partially. Believing God, trusting him and accepting that truth became my filter, my way of thinking. I would base my life and my decisions on this. It would prove to be priceless. And it was just the beginning of my journey. I, too, would need to be a seeker, to chase after God and find the pearls along the way.

In Matthew 13:44 Jesus said, "The kingdom of heaven is like treasure hidden in a field. When a man found it, he hid it again, and then in his joy went and sold all he had and bought that field."

TWO

Authority of the Believing Child

"Let the little children come to me and do not
hinder them, for the kingdom of heaven
belongs to such as these."
—Matthew 19:14

One of the first things I learned as a believer was that I
was given power in Jesus name to say NO and to tell the enemy to go away. If I had a bad dream or a bad thought my
parents taught me to use my authority as a believer. I was
given the words, I rebuke you Satan in the name of Jesus.
Satan or any other demon had to obey me because I was a
believer and spoke in Jesus name. I tried it out for myself
and it worked. It was around that same time when I was
only six or seven that my precious friend Kathleen told me
she was having nightmares. I quickly shared with her the
power she had as a believer to tell the enemy to go away in
Jesus name. She tried it out and it worked for her too. I
wasn't surprised!

Kathleen and I did just about everything together as
kids. Because I'm a year older, we jokingly say we've been
friends since she was born. Our parents were friends before
either one of us came into the world, so we were destined to
become BFFs (best friends forever). One warm Saturday

morning in June, we had a race. She was seven and I was eight at the time. I had just finished my chores and was finally out the door zooming down the main road through our town on my pink Huffy bicycle. Kathleen's long chestnut brown hair whipped through the air in front of me. She was tan, as usual, with natural highlights gleaming in the sun. She always looked like a GAP add without trying, a natural beauty. I, on the other hand, was slightly sunburned, with short wavy red hair. I sported the Dorothy Hamill professional ice skater hairstyle – it didn't require as much maintenance. Huge freckles covered my Irish American face. I could have been the poster child for the Irish Tourist Board. Squinting to keep my big blue eyes from drying out, I raced against the wind to get to the firehouse first. Kathleen was fast but so was I. We couldn't have been happier out and about on a warm summer day!

As we rushed into the empty firehouse parking lot, a young man in his 20s came walking out of the building. He was cute, very cute. We smiled and hit the brakes as he made his way over to our bikes. I could feel myself blushing slightly as he got closer. I thought for sure he'd go right to Kathleen. Then all of a sudden he sat right on my front tire and said, "What's your name little girl?" Without batting an eye I responded firmly, "Get off my bike, mister!" All the blushing left my face in an instant. He jumped up realizing he had crossed an invisible line, my line. I wasn't comfortable. He didn't have a line in his head but I sure did and I wasn't afraid to let him know. He had gotten into my personal space without my permission. Cute or no cute, I had developed a sense of what was appropriate. This just didn't feel right.

"Wow! You really told him!" Kathleen gleamed. "Huh, I guess I did?!" I even amazed myself. It felt really good, even powerful! It was true. Something clicked. I had the power to choose. I stood up for myself even though I was caught off guard and blushing. I had bounced back. Brave never felt so good.

That summer I was taking horseback riding lessons. I was in a corral by myself with the horse. We had been trotting along nicely when all of a sudden the horse got spooked and began to gallop. I was thrown to the side, barely holding onto the reins. Somehow my knees locked around the horse mainly out of fear. As he raced around the perimeter of the corral my head came within inches of the fence posts. The trainer tried to get a hold of him but it took multiple rounds before she was able to get the horse under control. I must say, it was the most fear I had ever experienced. When the trainer finally pulled me off I was shaken to the core. My whole body trembled. I was beyond tears and in a state of shock. She tried to comfort me but I was done. All I wanted was to get to safety, away from that horse. Standing there in a daze it finally dawned on me that I was okay. I didn't get hurt after all. I sobbed as I realized how close I was to getting killed. And then the trainer made the most unthinkable statement. "Fiona, you have to get back up on this horse". I shook my head. "No way! Maybe another horse in a few years but never that horse. I will never get on that horse again". And then she said, "If you do not get back on this horse you will be afraid of horses for the rest of your life."

I stood there crying and struggling internally. It was hard, very hard but I could see clearly what the trainer was talking about. I would end up carrying this fear for the rest of my life. I didn't want fear to win. I wanted to be free. And so after taking a moment to calm down I chose to come against that fear and get back up. I didn't like it but I did it anyway. I can't say I felt perfectly peaceful but I definitely overcame the fear. It was a hard lesson; one I hadn't planned to learn that day. I'm so thankful I got back up because I really love horses and I would have missed a lot of precious moments in my future. This was just the beginning. God would prove to use everything in life to make me stronger.

That year I was given pearls for the first time by a family friend. I was a flower girl in her wedding. I couldn't believe she was giving me a real pearl necklace. I felt so very special wearing it. It was an extravagant gift for an eight year old and I was all too aware. I knew pearls were costly and dear. To make a whole necklace you had to find the exact same size pearls that were perfectly rounded. My mother told me their story, how they begin their formation from a single grain of sand during moments of irritation inside the oyster. It's amazing that something so beautiful can come from an irritation. Just like the fellow who sat on my tire or the spooked horse, these irritations became moments of truth that turned into pearls I could wear for the rest of my life. I didn't like it at the time but I loved what came out of it. It became part of my treasure box.

Pearl Power

You're stronger than you think! Kick fear out and let faith in. "I can do all things through Christ who gives me strength." — Philippians 4:13

Discernment, My Super Power

We do have the power to choose. Not only can we choose how we handle situations with other people but we have the power to choose how we handle our own thoughts.

We decide what can stay and what has to go. Our thought life is the most private thing we have. Choosing good thinking leads to good actions.

I may have been eight or nine at the time when I had the most unusual experience. It was truly insidious. I understand it all a lot better now but when it happened I didn't realize how profound the attack was on my life and my destiny. I was playing alone in my bedroom, which I shared with my older sister Siobhan (pronounced Shavon, I told you we were Irish). I remember walking from my bed to my dresser when all of a sudden a thought came. It was loud in my head and stopped me in my tracks: "I wonder if I'm straight?" I didn't even know what those words meant at the time. It seemed very strange that words would come to my mind that I didn't understand or initiate. "What does *straight* mean anyway?" I thought. And the fact that it came in first person... "I wonder if **I'm** straight?" It was as if I was talking to myself and questioning myself. But how could I ask myself something I was not familiar with? At the same time it felt like I was being questioned. My spirit felt disturbed. Something about those words just didn't seem right. They weren't my words. I decided to drop it cold. I simply stopped giving it attention and went back to what I was doing. It was by the grace of God those words did not take root.

The truth was that I didn't really love all the typical girly things. I wasn't into shopping, dresses, or ballet. My favorite colors were green and blue not pink and purple. I liked dolls but that was mainly just for giving them a haircut. I would rather be outside climbing a tree, chasing the boys, or on some adventure. I could identify with Maria from the Sound of Music, running to some mountaintop to be surrounded by nature and singing her little heart out! She wasn't typical either. She had short hair, climbed trees, rowed boats, raced bikes, roamed creation, and loved God.

She didn't seem too concerned about her appearance as she wore the one dress the poor didn't want. She took care of herself but wasn't trying to impress anyone. Seems to me she found her bravery first and later discovered her beauty when she and the captain fell in love; and, on she went with her brave and beautiful life. Sounded good to me! I loved Swiss Family Robinson, The Apple Dumpling Gang and Anne of Green Gables. Girls took time growing into themselves and one day, almost suddenly, became the beauties they had hoped to be all along.

I had a piece of my brave but I was still growing into my beautiful. I believed one day I would find it. But for the time being I would need to grow into my big front teeth, accept my changing body, and learn to love myself for just being me. There was no comparing myself to a Barbie doll. I just didn't look like that. I was myself, complete with short bright red hair, loud freckles, and sparkling blue eyes. I had a passion for life, for God, and for adventure. This was good! God even said it was good when he thought of me. He was the one who made me and he knew exactly what he was doing... no mistakes.

It wasn't until years later that I learned what *straight* meant. I was amazed that the enemy tried to confuse me so early. By the grace of God I didn't question myself, my gender, or my sexuality. I also learned a huge lesson in how the enemy operates. Oftentimes when the enemy, who is also known as the accuser, is trying to plant seeds of destruction, he will put thoughts in our minds that come in first person. In truth, it is the enemy speaking the lies but he makes it sound like you are saying it to yourself. For example, instead of saying, "**You're** a failure," he'll plant the thought "**I'm** a failure." So, it sounds like you came up with the idea when it's really the dirty devil. He hates us. He not only plants the thought, but he also accuses us of having it.

Talk about evil! He hates that we are made in God's image and likeness. The devil will try anything to get us off base. "He comes to steal, kill and destroy" (John 10:10 NIV). He'll try to mess with our identity, our faith, and our trust in God just like he did in the garden with Adam and Eve. He was trying to plant seeds of doubt so they would question their God, their faith, and their identity.

The amazing thing about being a child and being a believer is that you are given the same tools as an adult. You don't get a junior Holy Spirit. You get *the* Holy Spirit. You can tell when the enemy is up to no good and decide against him; say *no*, and put up a wall. It's called discernment. **Your spirit has a radar. It tells you what's safe and what's not, like hot and cold. You can reject lies and push back, putting things where they belong in your head and in your heart. When you do, you create convictions.** The more you push back the stronger your convictions get and the stronger you get. Pretty powerful and pretty cool, especially for a child!

Everyone loves superheroes. Discernment gives you the opportunity to *be one* because it's actually a supernatural power! The Bible says in II Peter 1:3 NIV, "His divine power has given you everything you need for life and godliness." It's God speaking to you, directing you and giving you strength to do what's best. You can figure out what's right and then make great choices on a daily basis by listening to the Holy Spirit and pushing back the enemy. Of course this is all in the practice-makes-perfect category. It takes practice listening to God and paying attention to discernment. But it works! I didn't get it all right all the time but I was practicing!

Not Pot

Another foundational moment I remember quite vividly came soon after. It happened on an autumn afternoon. My mom had asked me to pick up a gallon of milk at the neighborhood market. As I made my way down the trail behind the store I could see a teenager leaning on the cement wall that led to the front of the building. Sometimes kids were up to no good back there. I felt cautious but also confident. I could hold my own. As I got closer I noticed he was struggling to stand up; it looked as if he had both vomited and urinated on himself and was completely emaciated, scary skinny. I'll never forget his words, "You wanna buy some pot?" I was shocked. I couldn't believe he was trying to sell me drugs. I was still a child. He must have been extremely desperate. It was very sad to me that he was trying to sell the very thing that made him look this way. I could see the dark side of giving in to such a temptation. It was actually scary to think of losing my life to something so worthless. I truly felt sorry for him. My heart was heavy. I didn't say a word and made my way around the corner. It was solidified. I could check that off. **I would never do drugs. It was one more conviction in my treasure box.**

Pearl Power

You don't have to wait until you get older to make great choices for your life. You can decide as a child what are good wholesome steps to make. God will help you understand what's best. "Folly delights a man who lacks judgment, but a man of understanding keeps a straight course." —Proverbs 15:21

Getting to Church

Many important choices that would form my life came early, between 11 and 14. I needed to know what I believed, where I was heading, and what my convictions were. If I didn't have any particular convictions on a major issue I needed to get them quickly. Life was coming at me fast. The way I thought about God, my world and myself would play a huge part in what happened in high school and beyond. Those were tricky years. Sometimes I felt steady and sometimes extremely vulnerable – getting to church, getting to God in worship, and being around other believers really helped. I needed to be around faith, and more than just my own.

We had church services Sunday morning and evening as well as Wednesday night, and youth group on Friday. I tried to get there as often as possible. Sometimes it was hard on Wednesdays because of school but when I would make the extra effort God always met me in a special way. One thing I loved about church was meeting missionaries and hearing all the crazy God-stories. I longed for the same for my own life. I thought it would be amazing if God would use me like that one day. Sometimes we would have the traveling ministers stay at our home. Sitting at the table and listening to all the awesome and powerful miracles were inspiring. My spirit would get fired up and amazed by God and how he uses all kinds of people. I noticed they were all very real and down to earth. What made them stand out was their willingness to just do what God told them to do. The joy of following Jesus was absolutely contagious. These people were having fun!

I remember this one young handsome missionary couple. They had such a passion for God, perfectly blended with an outrageous sense of humor about life. I'll never forget a story they shared about a couple that went skiing in Vermont. They were beginners. After taking a lesson on the bunny hill and learning how to snowplow for braking, they were off to the five-mile trails. They loved it. It was a perfect day for skiing. After many flawless runs they had once again gotten dropped off at the top when the wife realized she had to use the restroom and was not going to be able to wait until they reached the ski lodge. The husband said it was no problem. She could just shimmy herself over behind a big rock and he would distract anyone who came by. She took his advice and made her way behind the bolder. She dropped her trousers, assumed the position but with that slipped back on the skis and began sliding out from behind the big stone. Her husband saw her shoot out on the trail like a bar of wet soap. He shouted, "Honey, what are you doing?" She yelled, "I slipped! Help!" But unfortunately she had a perfectly aerodynamic position and was flying down the trail, bumping her poor little bottom as she went. He couldn't catch up to her speed as she whipped down the slopes only to find herself right in front of the lodge, pants down. It was an awfully embarrassing moment.

An ambulance was called and she was laid on a stretcher awaiting her emergency vehicle in the first aid room. All of a sudden another fellow was brought in on a stretcher as well. This guy was really messed up. They didn't even want to ask what happened because of all his moaning – it looked like he had a broken leg *and* a broken arm. The man decided to tell them what happened. He said, "You'll never believe it. I was in the ski lift when all of a sudden I saw a lady skiing down the trail half naked. I leaned over in disbelief and slipped right out of the lift!" "Oh we believe it!" they said. The next day they all were in the papers.

We laughed so hard! I loved them even more for being so real with us. I could see their genuine fulfillment in ministry and a deep love for God and people. They told us what went right and what went wrong and how God carried them through. Everything worked out as they trusted God. I loved their transparency and how they didn't have to appear like they had it all together. They just wanted us to know how much God had it together and they were following him. They were only in their 20s! Perfect! I got a vision! I could see myself going to South America in my 20s. Adventure was out there!

Pearl Power

You are never too young or too old to get a vision for your life. Getting a vision for your self is very important to God. The way you see yourself is what you will become. You can change the way you see yourself by changing your vision. God believes in vision so much that he said, "Without a vision the people perish." Ask him what he thinks about you and believe his words.

Need to Know Basis

I was always on more of a "need to know" basis about things... still am. I didn't have to be "in the know" and really wasn't too concerned about it either. I figured if I needed to know something then I would. I had questions but there wasn't any major prying on my part to figure life out all too quickly. Some questions seemed a bit out of my space and timing. I enjoyed living presently and felt a nice rhythm of growing as it happened. I believe my parents were wise not to give me too much information too soon. They knew life would happen, it was inevitable; they didn't try to explain it all. That was good for me. Sometimes too much information too early can cause curiosity and concern about things that are not present. I didn't need that. I also realized I could push the stop button on information... and I did need that. My thoughts were the most private thing I had. I wanted them uncluttered and some things were just not meant to be shared with someone so young. It's good to be innocent, to not know everything. The Bible says in Titus 1:15, "To the pure all things are pure, but to those who are corrupted and do not believe, nothing is pure. In fact, both their minds and consciences are corrupted." When I focused on things that were good, healthy, and innocent, I would see things that way. I actually kept my head out of trouble by not knowing so much about worldly things. When negative, impure, or unhealthy thoughts came, they stuck out and there was a choice. The best choice for me was to just flush them. Yes, just like in the bathroom! They were not worth keeping around and would only stink up the rest of my thoughts.

Pearl Power

"A simple man believes anything but a prudent man gives thought to his steps" —Proverbs 14:15. Think about what really matters; extra unnecessary information or a clean and clear thought life? You can get a whole lot more accomplished with an uncluttered mind. It's that simple!

The Truth about Projection

My dad had a doctor interning at his practice. She was lovely, a friend of the family and a believer. She had been in many pageants and had even won a state competition heading towards Miss USA. She was staying with our family for a few months so there was lots of opportunity for conversation. I remember helping myself to a nice big bowl of ice cream and sitting down with her one afternoon. It was during one of my growth spurts. I was a little chubby just before hitting all my changes and then I grew like a weed. It didn't matter what I ate. I could run it off in 10 minutes. When I sat down she looked at me and then looked at the big bowl. Then leaning over she whispered, "Do you have a problem with bulimia?" I leaned in and said, "What's that?" She said, "It's when you throw up your food after you eat so you don't gain weight." I was a little shocked by the definition and uncomfortably said, "No." I didn't know people did such things. It certainly didn't sound like a good idea. She looked at me suspiciously and said, "Are you sure? That's a lot of ice cream!" I couldn't believe she thought I would lie about such a thing. I was a kid for crying out loud! What kid doesn't love ice cream? But the thing that bothered me the most was that she didn't believe me. She even went to my parents to tell them about her concerns. They assured her I was fine and never made me feel worried or doubted. For that I am grateful.

I really had to stand up for myself on the inside and not let her words get to me. I didn't like being questioned like that. I didn't like the suspicion. I had to stick to the truth of what I did know. The truth was my freedom. And if there is a question posed, I have the freedom to not go down the road of "what ifs." I could have let it run me down, asking myself: "What if I could have that problem?" "What is all that anyway?" "Why did she think that?" Blah, blah, blah! I just didn't need to know another thing about bulimia. I didn't have a problem and I certainly didn't need one.

What I wasn't aware of at the time was that this lady actually had a problem herself. She struggled with an eating disorder and she was projecting it on me. She was trying to find her problem in me.

Pearl Power

It is a great freedom when we can state with clarity who we really are. We don't need to get entangled in someone else's words just because they seem like they should know what they are talking about. We can be brave enough to stay true to ourselves. Our identity is not up for grabs. We can shake off other people's words if they are not edifying or speaking life into our future. There's no reason to carry someone else's baggage. We will have our own struggles to contend with. No need in adding extra. Besides, "It was for freedom that Christ has set us free" Galatians 5:1. God wants us free, free, FREE!

Big Little Sister

By the time I was five I had reached the same height as my sister, Siobhan, who was two years older. I never had the joy of hand-me-downs. We shared the same size for years and eventually I began inching my way up. I marveled at my mother and sisters who remained petite at the five-foot marker. They marveled at me as I eventually grew 6 ½ inches taller and became the big little sister. Needless to say, Siobhan and I didn't always see things eye-to-eye (pun intended). We shared a bedroom for more than a decade. Siobhan would frequently ask if I would like her to tickle my back with the contingency that I would reciprocate. I always agreed gladly considering Siobhan kept her nails long and perfectly filed for the task. It was more of a special talent. She loved tickling all the children's backs – it was kind of like her own little love language. But it was far from fair. I had the habit of biting my nails and she never knew what she was in for. Besides, I would take full advantage of her special gifting and pretend to fall asleep before keeping my side of the deal. Just not right!

Siobhan also had this amazing ability to save candy in her top dresser drawer. I, on the other hand, would eat mine as quickly as possible. There was no savoring or saving to be had. It only left me longing for more. This was troublesome and led to my craving downfall. I would "happen to stumble upon" these sweet little well-hidden morsels. Yes, I loved her but I loved candy too. The temptation was much too great. I fell every time. Pitiful! If it had been my stash that was preyed upon I would have been raving mad. She saved for months only to discover an empty drawer! Oh the betrayal!

Seeing eye-to-eye was tricky on many levels. Siobhan was no pushover. She had a tremendous sense of purpose and leadership even at a young age. She loved doing everything with excellence and precision and could do just about anything she put her mind to. Her side of the room was always kept neat and in order. She was literally in childhood character training to become a great doctor, phenomenal wife, mother of six, and a powerful woman of God. She would need to be strong, indeed! I nonetheless was this free spirited, whimsical, light-hearted soul. My joy was to turn everything into a song, a dance, an accent, or a joke. I didn't have to break the ice as my older siblings did. They really plowed a nice, level path before me and my personality was quite the contrast. Yes, I would be mighty in the land but I came in on a different angle.

Like every large family, there was a pecking order. Some pecked harder than others. I had two older siblings and two younger; but, I didn't like to peck. I wasn't looking for a fight even if I had a good reason to. As a matter of fact when there was a fight in progress and I happened to be a part, I would just go for cover. Put my hands up, shield myself, and wait for it to pass. This was how I coped. I felt overpowered at times but never the victim. I remained a free bird. I just didn't have the desire to fight back. One unassuming day I remember standing by the sink in the bathroom. Something happened that ticked my sister off; but, this time it was very different. As I looked down at her I had an epiphany. I was looking down! By this time I was five inches taller than she. FIVE inches!

"What? I'm taller. Why am I going for cover? Why don't I stand up for myself? I'm no wimp! Enough is enough! Do something, Fiona!" I thought. So, I picked her up and threw her down the hall. She hit a door and slid to the floor shocked and bewildered. Neither one of us knew what had gotten into me. She screamed, "MOM!" My mother came running up the stairs surprised to see her on the floor and me standing up unscathed. "What happened?" she questioned with a slight hint of astonishment.

Siobhan quickly informed her that I had picked her up and thrown her down the hall! Her eyebrows lifted in surprise and she responded smoothly, "Well... I hope you've learned your lesson" and walked away. That was that.

Our differences didn't end that day, but the fear did. There were still times when we disagreed, but I would no longer go for cover. I held my own. Standing steady, arms down, chin up, and reminding myself of who I was... a little bit taller, the big little sister.

Pearl Power

"You then, my son, be strong in the grace that is in Christ Jesus" —II Timothy 2:1. There is a time when God gives you grace to be strong to face your fear and to overcome. Just take it. You were not meant to be a doormat. You need to respect and esteem yourself no matter how the people around you are acting. Hold your own. Take the grace and be strong.

(I have to confess, I never even considered sharing this story as I have the utmost respect and honor for Siobhan; but, she suggested I tell it knowing it could bring healing to others. We love each other deeply from the heart. God, in his infinite grace, brought sweet healing and restoration to our relationship. I absolutely cherish our sisterhood. I bless you my sister!)

Tight Jeans

One day as I was running out of the house to hop in the car and go to youth group when my dad stopped me on the driveway.

"You can't go like that," he said hesitantly.

"Like what?"

"You just can't go like that," he repeated with a very concerned look on his face.

I had never seen this look before. Peering down cautiously at the jeans that were glued around my lower region, he stated emphatically that I would need to change my pants. I had just gotten them that month and was so excited to get semi-dressed up for youth group. They were light blue with thin white stripes and my shirt was soft yellow with white stripes. I felt really good about the whole thing. I told him I had just gotten them.

He asked what happened. I wasn't quite sure what the problem was. I told him I was growing and they might have shrunk a bit in the dryer? He graciously said he was sorry and asked me to return to the house to talk with him for a minute. I was really disappointed but I could see it was a very big deal to him and he was trying desperately to explain something to me but didn't quite have all the words. Sitting down on the couch I was delayed a moment as it took me a second to lower myself. I had really shoved myself into these jeans. We both felt awkward and slightly embarrassed to have this conversation but I was really oblivious and he was really my dad.

He tried so hard to explain how it wasn't a good idea to wear tight things. He kind of mentioned how it wasn't good for other people to see me this way, boys in particular, and then tried to explain some things about when he was a teenager and a girl he knew that did this kind of thing and how that wasn't really good and we got more embarrassed the more he talked. I'm pretty sure both of our faces were red at this point. He finally brought it to a close. We were both relieved that it was over and I basically got the idea that it just wasn't right and that he cared enough to stop everything to tell me. That was enough for me. I know he didn't want me to be self-conscious but he did want me to know it wasn't the same for girls as it was for boys. For me it was a minor fashion mishap. For him it was a protection issue and a need to cover me, to guide my 12-year-old heart because I really didn't know how my fashion choices affected others. I was just beginning to learn about modesty and had just started noticing men noticing me. Once you notice their noticing, it's good to know what's modest because no one needs inappropriate attention. It only breeds inappropriate actions and that was not what I wanted.

It didn't feel good getting corrected by my dad but when I looked at the scripture, "My son, do not make light of the Lord's discipline, and do not lose heart when he rebukes you, because the Lord disciplines those he loves" (Hebrews 12:5-6a), I realize he was doing this because he loved me. That took courage. Now that I knew it was an issue it was my job to take care of myself whether my dad was watching or not.

I started to understand what good attention looked like. Sure there are people who have their own issues no matter what you're wearing. It's not my job to make sure everyone is thinking right; but, I can dress beautifully and avoid attracting negative attention to myself. This would bring me right back to discernment, my superpower! I could check in with the Holy Spirit and ask if I was in the zone... the "modesty zone." I found that I had more confidence and less distraction when I was in "the zone." I also felt like I was respecting myself and respecting the boys when I made good choices. Everybody likes some respect!

All this was a process. I still liked getting attention. I needed to figure out how that was supposed to look for a young girl. I would ask the Holy Spirit if there was a question in the back of my head about what I was wearing. It's just one of the sweet ways God tenderly leads us as women and women-in-the-making.

A few years later I found a verse that settled it all for me. I quickly wrote it down in my journal. Proverbs 11:22 "Like a gold ring in a pig's snout is a beautiful woman who shows no discretion". Yikes! There is no way I want to be that ring in the pig's nose. I am beautiful because God made me. I'm not looking to be displayed by something that rolls around in the dirt. Jesus please help me stay away from the pigs!

Pearl Power

Your spirit has a radar called discernment. It helps you to distinguish the truth from a lie. It encourages you to make accurate judgments of yourself and what is going on around you. It gives you the ability to choose wisely and to question a situation when necessary. The more you use it the stronger it becomes. Discernment comes directly from the Holy Spirit. Yielding to God's promptings causes your discernment to grow. He wants to preserve you, protect you and bless you. You will never regret following his leading. He is the Spirit of Truth.

THREE

One Miracle Will Do

"But he was pierced for our transgressions,
he was crushed for our iniquities; the punishment
that brought us peace was upon him,
and by his wounds we are healed."
—Isaiah 53:5

Life was moving along beautifully. We were very blessed as a family. My father's clinic was thriving. Our faith was strong and life was good. Seventh grade was behind me now and it was summertime. Woohoo! I rode my bike to Vacation Bible School at the local Baptist church and called home to check on the "baby status." My mother was in labor with the long awaited baby number five, Deirdre Kaitrin. She was a promise they held in their hearts for nine years. A group of close friends from church had been praying in the living room all night as we awaited the homebirth; but, when the baby didn't come by morning, I was off to the next best thing, VBS.

"So what's the status?" I asked on the church pay phone.

"She's here."

"Are you kidding?" I thought it was my sister teasing me.

"No Fiona. This is Mrs. Kniskern. Your mother has delivered a beautiful baby...."

I dropped the phone and jumped on my bike, riding home like the speed of light. Kathleen, my friend who was with me, tried to keep up but it was no good. I had enough adrenaline to get us both home in warp speed. There she was, a magnificent 11-pound baby girl. My mother looked like an angel. Her face was glowing with joy. Everyone was filled with awe and wonder. Each baby is such a miracle. It's an amazing opportunity for children to witness the glory of God in such little hands and feet. For days we floated on sheer amazement.

It was only 12 days later when life took a major shift. We received a call that Kieran, my oldest brother who was 15 at the time, had been in a diving accident at a nearby lake. My father recalls hearing the ambulance outside his office window as my mother shared the news on the phone. He immediately rushed to the hospital but was surprised to find that the ambulance had not yet arrived. Finally, when the ambulance rounded the corner very slowly, my father realized the severity of the accident. Slow ambulances are typically indicative of a spinal cord injury. Being a doctor himself and specializing in the spine, my dad knew what they were up against. It was not looking good. Kieran had fractured his fifth and sixth cervical vertebrae; he was paralyzed.

After hearing the prognosis, my parents called us together as a family. They explained the situation but quickly reminded us of our faith and told us that we should all believe God at his Word and trust him to heal Kieran. We had heard so many testimonies of the miraculous and believed as a family that God is the healer and he still heals today, just like he did in Bible times. Then Dad, very emphatically, spoke of the power of agreement and urged us to stay together in faith. We agreed. He made it clear that if other people were speaking negatively about the situation that we should do as much as we could to remove ourselves from the conversation. It was more important to stay in faith and speak words of life. With that, my parents placed scriptures on the ceiling and floor of my brother's hospital room. He was in traction, four hours looking up and four hours looking down. Everywhere Kieran looked he could see posters of people walking and running; these life-pictures and scriptures of God's healing power would solidify his faith. The one I remember the most was Psalms 116:9 ESV, "I will walk before the Lord in the land of the living."

It was a serious time. Although, as a child, I don't remember feeling overwhelmed. We were resolved to see Kieran healed. The days became weeks and the weeks, months. Every morning my father would travel to the hospital before work. He said he usually cried all the way to Connecticut, praying in his prayer language because that's all he knew to do. He would pray his boldest prayers over Kieran and speak healing scriptures, giving Kieran vision and encouragement. Then he would massage Kieran's hands open because the atrophy had become so profound. It was hard to see Kieran going through so much. Every day was a tremendous challenge. Before the accident he was the picture of health, a very strong, muscular teenager who loved to work out and play football; but, in just a couple of weeks everything started to change. He lost weight and muscle tone and had to find ways to keep his heart and mind in the right place. My parents kept trusting God. They asked everyone they knew to pray and they kept a round-the-clock prayer chain.

I'll never forget sitting in church one Sunday when our pastor called out to my dad asking how Kieran was. Dad stood up with tears streaming down his face and declared, "Jesus Christ is Lord" and then just took his seat. Immediately the service turned into a prayer meeting and everyone from young to old was on their knees crying out to God for healing. We believed wholeheartedly that God had done it before and could do it again; yet, it seemed like things were getting worse.

One day my brother decided to ask God for himself if he would heal him or not. There was a light on the wall that could only be turned on by the patient pressing a certain button. He prayed, "Lord, if you are going to heal me, turn that light on." Before he could blink the light turned green. He just needed a confirmation, something that would sustain him. God was more than happy to oblige!

The road was rough. The days grew longer. Still Kieran and my parents were convinced to wait on God. At one point the doctors were pushing for surgery. I say pushing because they actually tried to prep him without my parent's permission. They wanted to fuse his neck so that he could touch a button with his tongue and move an electric wheelchair. That was far from what my family was believing for. It got a bit sticky and my folks weren't exactly their favorite people to speak with. They would sit down with my parents around a big conference table with a large group of doctors and tell my parents they were in denial and that they had to get a grip. Every time they spoke something negative over Kieran my dad would say "cancel" under his breath. He wouldn't receive those words and he wanted to break their power. Truly, "death and life are in the power of the tongue" just as Proverbs 18:21 says. He knew he would have to combat the negative words and speak life. "Cancel" meant he wasn't accepting what the doctors spoke over Kieran and those words could not take root. The doctors would get even more infuriated when my parents didn't accept their words but Mom and Dad were resolved to trust God, not man. They were relying on God to bring the healing. This was not going to be a natural occurrence. They would need the intervention of the Almighty. And they believed he would surely do it.

And then on one unassuming day, more than four months after the accident, at heaven's orchestrated moment Kieran moved! They were small movements but nonetheless movement! The doctors came to see what he was talking about but when they did he was already worn out and they called it spasms. So the next day he saved his energy and was able to show them all that he could do. Their jaws dropped and they shouted, "Get this boy to rehab! We will never doubt you Holy Rollers again!" God was working it out from the time we started praying four months earlier, but one day the healing came in a "suddenly!" All of a sudden something started, something changed; it was a true miracle. God healed my brother! The doctors were amazed. It even hit the local papers. It came little by little; yet, it was important to rejoice over the little movements as well as the big ones like when he took his first steps. It was movement small or big! And going from paralyzed to not paralyzed was pretty awesome! Kieran is now married, has two beautiful children, and works in that same hospital giving hope to people who are coming through spinal injuries as he did. Isn't God amazing!

This miracle shaped my life in so many ways. I realized at age 12 that I could ask God for anything. Nothing was too difficult! I could pray my own biggest, boldest prayers about anything in my life and God was listening and responding. I could stand on Scripture and believe God for impossible things because this was MY God! Throughout life I would come back to this miracle and remember what God had done – remember all the prayers, scriptures and faith that could move mountains. And most importantly, I too could wait on God, knowing every good thing is worth the wait. I didn't want to miss the blessing! I could say, with confidence, it was true; God does miracles today, not just back in Bible times. We believed. We asked. We stayed in faith. He responded and nothing would be the same. I'm so grateful my parents stayed the course of faith. It was quite a test but Kieran's life is an awesome picture of God's faithfulness.

Pearl Power

There is power in Scripture, speaking the promises of God and choosing to speak only words that go along with what we are believing for. It makes a difference. For my brother it was the difference between being paralyzed and walking. In life there are many situations that we can believe God for. We don't know what God will do but it is our privilege to ask and to believe. We honor God when we pray big bold prayers and ask for what is impossible with man. "For with God, all things are possible."

The Blessing

I didn't want to miss any of God's blessings. This led me to stop and really consider God's plan for my life. If God had a plan and I knew he did, then that included my husband. This was huge! Who I married was the most important decision of my life apart from giving my heart to Jesus.

It was the same year as the accident that I decided to sign an agreement with my dad about dating, courting, engagement and marriage. I had gone to a youth conference where they suggested having accountability with your parents. They even had a special covenant paper for dads and daughters to sign together. I brought a copy home with good intentions but left it sitting on my dresser. A few months passed and one day I felt a tug on my heart. It felt like a conviction. God was reminding me once again how important it was to have this covenant in writing. I needed to commit to it. It was a big deal for me to sign it. I didn't take it lightly. In signing I chose to only marry with my dad's blessing and save myself for that person. *Saving myself* meant holding hands and maybe kissing, but nothing else before the wedding. Nada, zilch, nothing! Even the kissing part would have to be limited. That stuff gets out of hand too. The blessing was my dad's approval, consent, and covering before God just like in the Old Testament. He would keep me from any and all unqualified individuals. This gave me great security and felt very settling. I needed that!

You wonder, why at 12? It may sound young but I had to choose where I would land before I got tested. I'm sure you could be even younger to make this determination and I would encourage that. It was so good for me to take a stand in my preteen state before all my emotions mixed with hormones could draw me in a different direction. I had no plans of dating any time soon and I had my mind made up to get my dad's blessing.

It actually felt really good, like it was just the right thing to do. I had a conviction and I had peace. That was enough. It was more than just a good idea; it was a God-idea. It was based on truth. He said to keep myself for one person. I was meant to give myself completely to one man within the boundaries of a covenant with God, called marriage. Waiting for that covenant to take place before intimacy brings trust into a relationship. You are trusting God first and in turn trusting each other. It's another great way to show personal integrity and character. True intimacy is not based on sex. It is a place of trust and protection for two hearts at their most vulnerable state whether having sex or not. Giving myself away early would mean I wasn't trusting God and had taken things into my own hands. Sex outside of marriage is not true intimacy. There is no blessing in the union. It's not protected. It's a temporary thrill that can be very damaging to the heart, mind and body. Sex inside marriage is a building block. It makes the marriage stronger, it deepens the trust and it is not based on performance but acceptance. God said it and I believed it. He never failed me, he made me and he loved me. He must have had a really good reason for all this. Marriage, intimacy and sex were all his idea. He created it all. He would know best. I didn't have to have all the answers. I just had to trust him and be humble. Besides, nobody can bless like God can! Obedience brings blessing in every area of life.... EVERY area of life!

God was helping me be clear with myself about where I stood in my beliefs. I was starting to get a vision for what I wanted to see happen with my own life, who I wanted to be when I grew up, and where I was headed. I didn't have myself all figured out but I was getting a picture. If you don't decide what you believe and where you stand especially in your sexuality you could succumb to anything, basically wander. It's like walking into a test without studying or trying to bake a cake without a recipe. If you don't decide who you are and what your convictions are before you're tested, you very well might blow the test. Getting a vision for your life is like getting directions before you leave the house. When you get on the road you know what direction to head in and what your final destination is. I didn't want my life to turn into a big W.... for "Whatever." I would have to wrestle with my own worth, esteem, and identity just like everybody else but standing on my convictions seemed like a head start.

This wasn't going to be something I kept to myself. I would need to talk about my convictions and let my friends know too. It's amazing the respect you get when you have strong convictions (You know they're strong when you're willing to share them). Even if someone doesn't necessarily agree with you or hasn't made up their own mind, they will respect you for your decision. If they don't respect your convictions then you won't need their help or their input. You can stand alone with God. He's enough!

> "I have learned the secret of being content in any and every situation, whether well fed or hungry, whether living in plenty or in want. I can do everything through Him who gives me strength."
> —Philippians 4:12-13

Pearl Power

There is a blessing for those who wait. Happily Ever After is something only God can do. How do you want to see your life and your heart in 10 years? You can avoid a lot of pain and wasted emotions by trusting God with your heart. He has a beautiful plan. Today is a great day to start! It's not too late.

To High School and Beyond!

High school started, I loved the change. It felt significant. I was a little more confident, a little braver, and I felt a little more beautiful. I had grown tall and slender, grown my hair out, and learned to play with shiny lip gloss, blue eyeliner, eye shadow, and mascara! My freckles had softened, my smile had matured, and I had gained more of an opinion about my wardrobe. Also, I really liked boys, just about all of them! I played field hockey and enjoyed our church drama team. Oh the drama! I started voice lessons with a professional opera singer and started figuring myself out a bit more. Things were coming together for me. I realized I wasn't very competitive in field hockey. I didn't need to be the first one down the field but I liked the camaraderie and I was happy to be a part. My closest friends were still in youth group. They all attended other high schools. At my school, I didn't know anyone else that shared the same convictions or the same relationship with Jesus. I heard one girl talking about being a born again believer in the locker room one day but then some other things she said didn't really line up for me so I figured we weren't quite on the same page. I realized a lot of what I believed was very different from everybody else. But my love for people and my bubbly personality let me hang with just about anyone. I made friends easily. I wasn't a follower but I wasn't actually leading anyone either. I was still learning how to be led... by God that is.

Sneaking Out

Being a bubbly person had its pros and cons. Talking and connecting with people came easy. I just didn't realize how attractive a good conversation could be. There was also the flirting issue. It seemed so innocent until somehow the line was crossed and someone started getting attached emotionally.

Since the boys outnumbered the girls in the neighborhood, Sunday school, and now youth group, I always felt more comfortable hanging out with them. Besides, boys weren't competitive with girls and you never had to worry about jealousy or anything catty. It was just easier; the only catch was the flirting thing.

One of my buddies worked at the local grocery store. I would make it a point to talk to him whenever I picked things up for my mom. In the winter he worked outside in the Christmas tree lot and I would visit just to talk. He was really a great kid, had a good heart, and we enjoyed one another's conversation. He also had a moped. It wasn't exactly the quickest means of transportation, but it moved and I was impressed. Ha!

One day we decided to meet late that night. I snuck out around 11:00pm and he met me at the end of my street with his moped to go for a cruise. How we planned this without cell phones is beyond my comprehension, but we did. We took a ride around town and then he dropped me off at the end of my street again. I walked up to my house quietly, snuck around the backyard, and backed into the kitchen trying to make sure the door didn't make any noise. As I turned around I was extremely surprised to see my mother sitting very calmly at the counter with her teacup in hand and teapot full. She smiled and asked if I had a nice time...

"Hmmm?" I thought. This IS my mother, I snuck out, and she's calm. She's asking me how it went??? Huh?

"Yes, it was very nice," I responded.

"Where did you go?" she asked kindly.

"Just for a quick ride on Brian's moped. He met me at the bottom of the lane. He's a nice boy," I responded quite dumbfounded.

"Would you like some tea?" she asked smiling again.

"Oh, no thank you. I'm kind of tired." Uncomfortable, awkward... and tired, I thought. Is she for real?

Off to bed I went.

The next night I decided to meet Brian again. Wouldn't you know; my mother who was asleep when I left, happened to be up when I got back... in the kitchen... with her tea, again. Same conversation with a few more added details, and off to bed I went.

This lasted from about a Tuesday to a Friday. By Friday I was sitting down, drinking tea at midnight with her and sharing my heart. Finally my mother told me she was really kind of tired throughout the day and didn't know how many more nights she could keep this up… all very matter of fact like. No judgment, no accusations, no finger pointing. That alone kind of freaked me out. I didn't know how she knew I was up and about; she never spoke of it then. She simply loved me, let me talk, and stayed up as long as I was willing to be with her. It makes me cry now, knowing it was the Holy Spirit that woke her up, and how much she must have been praying and how much she needed to trust God with me. She knew I was kind of a free spirit and I believe she was trying to connect with me without breaking my spirit. A few cross words and I would have felt very ashamed and very bad about myself. Somehow she had the grace to just come around me gently and show unconditional love.

I decided I couldn't have her getting up like that every night. She was losing sleep. I was losing sleep and I was feeling like I was leading this boy on. His attachment was growing and I knew I couldn't really be his girlfriend. It wasn't what I believed. We weren't on the same page in our faith and I would be stealing emotions that didn't belong to me. I wanted God's will for my life. This just wasn't it and I needed to guard my heart and his. Once I drew the line and told him I couldn't be his girlfriend, I felt the freedom and peace of being obedient. I was uncluttered again and I could run my race with perseverance.

Pearl Power

There was a scripture that would come up during these years of waiting. "Above all else guard your heart because it is the well spring of life." The more I guarded my heart the more I realized how much actually needed to be guarded. There was a lot more to this heart of mine than what could be seen. If my heart was free the rest of my life seemed to follow. An un-encumbered heart is a great freedom for a teenager. You are strengthened by each choice you make to guard what is most precious, your heart.

The Call

While at church one Wednesday night when I was 15, I decided to go up to the front of the sanctuary after the service and pray quietly by the altar. I'm pretty sure I was responding to the evening's message although I can't really remember what it was about now. All I remember is kneeling on the floor in a corner, with my head bowed on a step, talking to God heart to heart. I asked if he wanted to use my life in ministry. It was simple and sincere. While praying I got this sense that he was asking me in return if I would be willing to do whatever he asked. I had every desire to please God. There was no twisting my wrist, no questions, no doubts or fears – just a sweet little *yes*. When I agreed I had this awesome sense that this was what it meant to be called into ministry. And somehow in my spirit I knew my ministry would be to the nations, especially Latin America. God wanted to do something special with my life. I just needed to be willing. I'm pretty sure a few tears followed and it was settled.

Like the story of Samuel in the Old Testament, God wasn't waiting until I grew up and understood the whole thing. He was simply calling. I must admit, I didn't really know what it all meant. I just knew I had a purpose. It came after the yes. He wanted to do something special with my life and it had to do with the nations, especially Latin America. I didn't speak Spanish but that didn't seem to hinder God from calling me - actually, I think I was almost failing

Spanish at the time. I didn't have a degree or even a clue about the ramifications; and, I wasn't even old enough to go on my first mission trip. It was an ordinary Wednesday night; I was fifteen and I was called.

Pearl Power

You don't have to wait to hear God calling you to respond to him. God is looking for willing hearts. You don't have to be the most talented, best looking or most intelligent for God to use your life. You just have to say yes. He can use you in any career, anywhere, and even at any age. He is not looking for perfect people. He's looking for willing hearts that he can mold.

FOUR

The Crossroad

"But because of his great love for us, God,
who is rich in mercy, made us alive with Christ
even when we were dead in transgressions—
it is by grace you have been saved."
—Ephesians 2:4-5

Pearl Power

There's always a crossroad in the life of a believer, a call to complete surrender. It's the greatest call of one's life. Letting go of what's temporary for what's eternal. Vision and passion are only truly complete with devotion, to love Jesus more than anything else and seek him daily.

It was the summer after my sophomore year of high school. Youth group rocked! Church was the place to be; I had gone to teen camp and came back with a fire and a passion to see other teens experience Jesus as I did. I wanted so much to lead others to Christ I wanted to see people receive salvation, healing, and freedom. Most of my youth group friends all went to the same high school. I liked the idea of being closer to them so I decided to change schools. Before the school year started I had visions of students getting off the bus and heading right for the flagpole to pray and read the Bible together. I was all excited about how God was going to use me in powerful ways. What I didn't know was that I was getting primed for the test of my youth!

I remember starting school and feeling so special. I was new but I had a lot of friends already; so, this afforded me some extra attention I didn't have to work for. I didn't mind that a bit. School started on a Wednesday. By Friday, everyone was talking about the parties going on that weekend. A couple of my youth group friends said they would meet me at the lake and we could check things out. Innocent enough, I thought. Maybe we would even get to share Jesus with them? Hmm?

Saturday night came; we met at the lake and piled into a friend's car. We heard about a party on the other side of town. As soon as we arrived it was obvious the atmosphere had changed. It was a typical bad high school party setting; an extremely crowded house, loud abrasive music, lots of couples hanging all over each other, beer bottles in hands and smoke filling the air. Not my cup of tea. My church friends and I were trying to keep it cool, hang low, and just mingle. I didn't move from my spot. There was this strange underlying pressure to blend in and pretend like everything was okay when it just wasn't. We all felt a bit uneasy and finally someone suggested we leave. I was relieved. So we headed back to the lake. When we arrived there were a lot more teens gathered and everyone was laughing and telling stories. It felt a lot cleaner and just plain fun. I recognized a bunch of the kids from school. They treated me like a great addition to their circle of friends. As it got later my youth group buddies suggested it was time to head home. I was agreeing with them when I heard some kids behind me. They yelled, "Hey, aren't you that new girl at school?" I smiled and they said, "Yeah, it's great to see you. You don't have to leave. Why don't you stay with us?" I started feeling this wonderful sense of belonging, acceptance, extra attention and a pull.

I tried to reason with myself: "Seems like a good way to reach out. Build friendship and trust." My folks were away so I figured hanging out a little longer wasn't going to get me in trouble. I could handle it. A group of them said they were going up to a house nearby and that I was welcome. *Welcome* sounded nice. I reasoned, "It won't be like that other nasty party, just a nice bunch of kids hanging out." I decided to go. My church friends were slightly surprised but turned and headed home. No questions asked.

I noticed a stirring in my spirit. I was in a crowd but still very much an individual who didn't necessarily think like everyone else. I was still guarded, but it started to get a little blurry. They wanted to be my friends and they were being really nice about it. I'll just make "friends" and off I went, red flags and all.

As soon as we arrived they began to play a simple silly game. The catch was, you mess up and you have to drink. I was sure I wasn't going to mess up. I told them I didn't drink. They laughed and said, "Of course not!" It all seemed very innocent. Everyone was being kind. No one was talking trash. Conversation was easy and there were lots of smiles, especially coming from this one guy. I thought to myself, "These are good people. They don't want to do the wrong thing. They're just having a little fun." And then I messed up...

A few hours later I was holding hands with "Mr. Smiley" and being led down a hallway to a bedroom. It's amazing how little it takes. I ignored a handful of cues from the Holy Spirit early on. There were so many tugs on my heart to stop but I brushed them off and kept thinking, "I'll be heading home soon." I felt the urge in my spirit to get going; but, somehow made light of those red flags and hushed whatever uneasiness I was discerning.

It wasn't God's fault that I was in this predicament. He had given me every opportunity to stop, turn around, and get home. I was deliberately choosing the acceptance of people over the gentle nudges of the Spirit of God. It wasn't until we got to the bedroom that I realized how deep a pit I had fallen into. I felt a great distance from God. I was being disobedient and I had walked out from under the umbrella of protection. My spirit was troubled. I'm pretty sure this guy wouldn't have minded a bit if I had given away what was most precious to me that night, my virginity. And to think, we didn't even know one another. We "liked" each other. This was not about love. It was a set up to steal. How could something that seemed so innocent, with seemingly kind-hearted people, be so ridden with destruction? The first party was so obviously worldly I got out the first chance I had. This one caught me off guard. Being *off guard* was my problem. It was not an obvious assault but more of a covert operation, silencers and all.

Pearl Power

Red flags can save your life. "For the waywardness of the simple will kill them, and the complacency of fools will destroy them; but whoever listens to me will live in safety and be at ease, without fear of harm." —Proverbs 1:32-33

Finally, I came to my senses. This was not the plan. This was not where I saw myself. This wasn't even the real me. It was not what I agreed to: **"The Paper, the Covenant, my Dad, my Future!"**

In my stupor, I smoothly distanced myself and got out of that bedroom before anything happened. My newfound "friend" followed me like a puppy. I didn't make any staunch objections to the situation, but I didn't volunteer anymore of my time either. I knew I needed to find my way home. A bunch of us crammed into a little car and off we went around town again until we finally found my home.

Guilt and Condemnation

I haven't seen many horror movies (Okay, I've seen three to be exact. That was more than enough for my imagination. I always felt so disturbed afterward. It would take a week to wear off; and, still there were certain images that would stick for life. So not worth it.) The reason I bring it up is because when I got home and finally lay down on my bed, it felt like a horror movie. I literally felt like the weight of guilt and condemnation was sucking me into my bed. It seemed like every demon out of hell had something to say and was pouncing on me. I was bombarded with shame and disgust. The words kept coming up, "And you call yourself a Christian?" It was the greatest demonic attack I had ever experienced. I felt questioned to my deepest core. The enemy acted like he had all the evidence he needed to shut me up and put me away. I crossed a line. Now I was out of God's will. Why should God listen to me now? I didn't have any answers. I wanted to beat myself up too. For every cruel assault on my character I added my own deafening inner screams of guilt and self-abasement. My own heart condemned me. I literally felt a weight on my body. It was the darkest night of my soul. I knew I needed God desperately but I was too exhausted to fight off the things that swirled around me. I just kept telling God how sorry I was until the sun finally came up and I fell asleep.

My sister called to me a few hours later, asking if I wanted to go to church. I couldn't even imagine strolling into church after a night like that. I had a bit of a hangover and I was still in a pretty big pit. Church was the last place I wanted to be seen. My face would tell all. I was a hypocrite. I wouldn't be able to worship God. How could I even pray? I told her I wasn't feeling well and she should go without me. Rolling over, I slept a few more hours.

Mercy

Then something very sweet and unexpected happened. It would change my life forever. I remember suddenly feeling the sunlight pouring into my room and over my face. It was stronger than usual. My whole room was lit up. I could feel God's presence. His mercies were beckoning me. I was surprised to be surrounded by such kindness. For all my filth, pride and independence, here was God giving me hope, peace of mind and a love that ran so deep it steadied me. I tried to explain myself to him, but it was as if he was saying softly, "Shhhhh... It's okay. I know." It was as though he didn't want me to retell it, knowing how embarrassed I was. Instead, he was looking for a way to reach my heart, to comfort me, and to give me a way out. It was mercy. Sweet undeserved mercy. He was surrounding me, holding me close, and working very carefully to restore my heart. He wanted me to know his great love in the midst of my failure and not just when I could get my act together. How tremendously humbling. He initiated love before I even asked. He was not ashamed of me. Now all I had to do was yield. What a God!

As I pulled myself up and leaned back on my pillow, the tears came flowing and flowing. I could finally release it all. Now these were tears of acceptance and forgiveness. The heaviness, the guilt and all the condemnation had left and the peace was back. It was as if God himself was sitting right beside me holding my hand. He was giving me the strength to move forward and make things right. There was no room for shame but every opportunity for change in such relentless love.

The first thing I knew I needed to take care of was this new boyfriend, "Mr. Smiley". I called him up and asked if we could talk. We met at the lake. He was smiling again but that only lasted until I explained how sorry I was for the way I acted the night before. He lost all facial expressions when I told him that I wasn't really being true to myself. I don't think he ever heard this before. He didn't quite know how to respond other than, "It's no big deal."

Pearl Power

Well guess what "Smiley?" It is a big deal! I am a big deal! Me, my life, my future, my body, my kids, my husband, my God! It's all big! I am not a toy. I am not a fling. I am not temporary entertainment. I am precious, dear, priceless, and treasured by God Almighty. It's big alright!

I knew it would be hard for him to understand what I was saying because he obviously didn't have the same convictions; but, it was important for me to face what I had done and clear the air. I was allowing myself to be sifted, to be set apart, to not be like the others and to identify the true me. Did I feel awkward? Totally. Did I feel a bit different from the rest? You bet. But did I feel free? YES! The most beautiful freedom! ! It didn't matter what "Smiley" thought, just what God thought. He had given me the courage and the grace to walk out my freedom and stand up for myself. There was a strength in my resolve and a peace that just wouldn't quit. I was amazed by myself!

That was a piece of cake compared to my next deep conversation. It's one thing to talk to someone you hardly know about how you really don't know each other; but, it's another thing to talk to people who really know you, especially your parents, about how you weren't being you and that you completely crashed. My parents would get home that afternoon. It was clear what God was asking me to do. I needed to tell them. Everything.

I thought about leaving some stuff out. I'm sure I didn't want to bring any *extra drama*. Besides, we should speak life, right? And this just wasn't all that edifying. It's tricky to be positive while considering the confession of one's downfall. This was going to be hard; but, it was all too spelled out. This was not about making things right with everyone else and trying to salvage my reputation. This was about being obedient to God and making things right with him; and, letting all the other pieces fall where they may.

Pearl Power

Have you ever had to do something or say something you knew would be hard and you knew would cause someone else pain but you still had to say it? It is not easy confronting your own failure before others, knowing they would be disappointed and that you had broken their trust. It's such a great test because the truth is you could avoid the talk and bury that little morsel of history; but, you will never be truly free until you confront it.

My parents came home. We shared heart to heart. I told them everything. They were upset. It was hard. Very hard. I had broken their trust. They were going to need time. They had their own reactions and their own way to handle it. I just had to hold on and trust God. But one thing I could be sure of was that I was taking steps of obedience and even in the pain of being the object of their disappointment I had a sense of peace and calm that everything would be alright. I was very sorry. They knew that. And, I was honest. They realized I chose to tell them. Now it was up to God. I would need his help to mend and heal our trust.

Pearl Power

There is nothing that can separate us from the love of God. He loves us no matter what. We will fail, but God will never fail us. He is always looking to restore us. He is not waiting to judge us. Guilt, condemnation, and shame do not come from him. These are the things the enemy uses to keep us from God's love. Our own hearts will condemn us but God is the strength of our hearts and our portion- just what we need when we need it. It takes a brave soul to trust God's love. His love can change it all.

Youth Pastors Rock

Later that evening I called my youth pastor, Rich Catapano. I asked if we could talk and set up a time for the next day. Yes, I should have been going to school but sometimes it's more important to go see your youth pastor!

He was so kind. I was a blubbering mess; but, it felt good to make my confession. He listened, prayed and then asked some really helpful questions that made me realize I was missing a pearl. I had passion, conviction, and vision; but, the one thing I didn't have established was my devotion. Of all the "tions" to be missing!

So he made a few suggestions that would help bring some order to my world and get my roots down a bit deeper. He told me to get a notebook and to start writing to Jesus – my prayers, questions, revelations, dreams, everything and anything. He told me to get hold of a Bible and make it my devotional Bible and then to choose a place I would go to everyday to be quiet with God. He then said to start reading my Bible in the book of John and read as much as I liked each day, as long as I read something. He told me to then write about it (What the passage means to me, how I could apply it to my life today and any questions I had about it.) and then offered to answer the questions that popped up to the best of his ability. Rich explained the concept of being a "branch." The branch can't do anything apart from the tree; but, as long as it's connected to the tree it can grow and bear fruit.

I had been doing some freelance Christianity, going to church and every big event; but, when it came to the daily walk I wasn't rooted. I wasn't looking to God to direct my steps throughout the day. I loved God and knew God had a plan for my life yet I wasn't seeking him for it. That's where devotion comes from – checking in with God and choosing to follow him daily. It's hard to follow someone you haven't talked to in a bit.

So, I started to write, and write, and write! I didn't realize how much I needed to talk to God and how much I would love sitting quietly in my room with my Bible and journal just having "Jesus time." The more I sat with him the more I could see clearly who he really was. The clearer he got, the clearer I got. And then I realized he had a lot to say too. It was definitely not a one-way conversation! I had to learn to pay attention to him. If I took the time to wait and listen there would come some instructions. This opened a whole new realm. Now I had to choose to do what he actually said. It brought a lot of things in life to light.

I realized I had some decisions to make. My motives were not the best for changing high schools in the first place. As I prayed I could feel God asking me to return to my previous school. Yikes! Grace took on new meaning that day. It was not only the unmerited favor of God but his strength that gets released in our obedience. A pearl indeed! I knew I had to do it and I did. Yes, I had to explain it to a lot of friends. I chose to tell the truth. It was my only option. In some miraculous way I didn't take on one drop of shame. Amazing grace indeed!

Now that I was seeking God and asking for help every morning before the day began, I could see things working out. I would run into the people I needed to see and share what I needed to share. I saw a few people from the party and I could feel the Holy Spirit gently nudge me and ask me to apologize to them. There was no embarrassment, just conviction. I remember running into two girls in the bathroom. They smiled and commented on how I was back at the old school. I smiled and told them I was so sorry for my actions that night and that I wasn't being true to myself. They smiled again yet kind of in shock, but said how it was really no big deal. After that I was just fine. They may have thought it was my parents' idea to send me back; but, that was between Jesus and me. It really made absolutely no sense to anyone who was trying to preserve the slightest semblance of being cool or hold onto the last smidge of their reputation. Yet somehow it made perfectly good sense to me because I had peace. Man! Peace goes a long way. Hurray for peace!

You can be ridiculously obedient when you know God has spoken directly to you and you've got peace! Being obedient is a lot easier once you're surrendered. I thought I was surrendered before. Now I knew I was. I completely laid down my whole life. I was feeling 100% free and 300% alive, body, mind and spirit!

Pearl Power

There is a time when you may feel separated from the people around you because of your faith and your convictions. You may have to stand alone. It is a test. When you put God first and take hard steps to stay on course there is an inexplicable joy and freedom that come. Freedom is worth the sacrifice! You will never regret it.

Getting to Know God

I looked forward to my time with God. I was amazed at how much he wanted to teach me. There was a scripture I read in the book of John where Jesus said, " I have much more to say to you, more than you can now bear. But when he, the spirit of truth, comes, he will guide you into all truth." (John 16:12-13) Jesus said this before he ascended to heaven. The Holy Spirit is God's presence on the earth. He would teach me and guide me into all truth. Every pearl I needed came from him, the spirit of truth. I was amazed at how clear things became. No more fuzz. Things made more sense. There was purpose even in things not working out because I was learning to trust God. Trust helped me bridge what I could see with what I couldn't. I started to grasp the sovereignty of God. When he said he would work it all together for good it was because he could see every detail start to finish. He had me strategically placed in time and history. Trusting him meant I would allow him to do whatever he saw best in his sovereignty, whether or not it made sense to me yet. Peace plowed the way. I could always trust his peace. It was like a traffic light. Red, no peace, stop. Green, peace, go!

I learned that God was just as concerned about me catching the little details as the big ones. Little things really mattered to him – little attitudes, little obediences, little whispers, little choices. He was testing to see how much I would pay attention. I never heard him audibly; but, I sure could hear that still, small voice. The more I paid attention, the louder it got.

I also learned that God loves little spaces. It still amazes me for such a big God. Sitting on my bed was nice; but, sitting on my floor in a corner, somewhat hidden, seemed like a secret place and he liked that. He said in Psalm 139:15 that before I was conceived he made me in a secret place. Secret places are precious to him. Since I loved blessing him I would try to find those spots. For me, to hide myself to meet with God felt special. Kind of funny, but true. That must be where the "prayer closet" concept comes from.

I started to learn that God cherished our times together. He wanted to share secrets with me, to reveal himself to me, to confide in me. He was watching my heart to see if he could trust me. It was obvious this was not a one-sided relationship. Trust would have to go both ways. It amazed me that he even longed to trust me too. He seemed to yearn for my trustworthiness so he could show me more of himself, bless me more from the inside out, and just pour out more of himself on me. He's such a love! Sometimes I would experience a truth about God and then find it later in Scripture. One day I read, "The Lord confides in those who fear him." (Psalm 25:14) I knew the truth before I read it. Pretty cool!

When we see the word "fear" we may think of its negative connotations but fearing God is actually the most positive way to use that word. In the Bible it doesn't mean to be scared or afraid of him so that we run away. It means to respect and revere him so that we come close. When angels showed up in Scripture the people always freaked out. The angels had come from God's presence and carried a measure of his glory. Can you imagine what we would do if God showed up in all his glory? Moses couldn't even look at him. He only saw his back as he passed him on the mountain and still Moses face was lit up so brightly that the people asked him to cover up so they could be around him. God is truly worthy of all our respect, reverence and awe. And when we spend time with him our faces can get a healthy glow too. People certainly recognize the difference.

I started taking walks with God, sitting at a nearby lake, talking to him about everything and anything. Sometimes I would get caught up and spend hours in my room reading, writing, praying, worshipping... just being with him. I could sense his presence in lots of different places. There are many ways that God speaks to us. One major way is through creation. That's one of my favorites. I loved applauding him for the beautiful details I noticed around me. I had a specific dock that I would meet him at by the lake. Just being still, quieting my soul and waiting, would speak volumes to my heart about who he was. I truly fell in love. The real stuff. The more I came to know God, the more I realized how very precious it was to be in a relationship with him. I was learning to trust him and he was learning to trust me.

Journaling became a journey. My first journals were left-over notebooks from high school. Yes, the ugly black and white ones, Spring Composition Books; but oh, how I treasure them! I love going back and reading my heart, remembering those painful struggles and inspiring victories, watching how God carefully led me with all my ups and downs, questions, and fears. I was just trying to work it out and that I did! Forty journals later my writing is the same after all these years – blessing God for the day, asking for help, praying for people, writing down new songs from my heart, asking questions, writing scriptures, venting, asking for forgiveness, direction, confirmation, or just admiring creation. It's so wonderful to be in conversation with my Creator!

From the earliest journal I could find:

Dear Father,

Please make me a prayer warrior for you. Cleanse and purify my life, fill me with your Holy Spirit, give me a song in my heart and a clear-cut message of your truth, and make me a person of prayer. I want to be like you. Open my eyes so I can see you and know you.

My song today:

Blessed is he whose sins are forgiven

Blessed is he whose heart has been broken

Blessed is he who desires to be chosen

And blessed is he whose life is the Lord's

Therefore, let everyone who's godly pray to you

Therefore let everyone who's holy stand for you

Therefore, let everyone who loves you say to you my God

You are the Lord of all

For his anger lasts only a moment

But his favor lasts a lifetime

Weeping may remain for a night

But rejoicing comes in the morning

Journal Notes:
Sunday, January 24, 1988

Dear Jesus,

Thank you for this day. It has been a real blessing to feel your presence and anointing in my life through prayer and ministry this morning. I

also want to thank you for the beautiful and encouraging people you spoke through to encourage me at
church.

Lord I give all the compliments and applause
to you as one big bouquet. This was only to glorify
your name.

Please make me like you. Help me do your
will no matter what the cost. Give me strength in
your word and in the power of prayer and devotion.

I love you Lord!

Pearl Power

God is looking for conversation with you. He wants to explain
faith, to share secrets, to reveal himself, to meet you in small special
places and help you understand what is most important in life. He
loves to be acknowledged in everyday situations, to be included and
welcomed. Life is completely different when you enter this kind of
relationship with God. It takes on a whole new meaning.

FIVE

Devotion and a little Drama

"Blessed is the man who listens to me, watching daily
at my doors, waiting at my doorway. For whoever finds me
finds life and receives favor from the Lord."
—Proverbs 8:34-35

This is where things started to take a turn in my life from cloudy to clear. Before, I had dreams and visions and lots of great ideas but there was still a wave of "what ifs" and a maze of options. I honestly didn't enjoy having too many options. It seemed confusing and added too much information. I just wanted to know what I should do and go do it. I believed if God was telling me to do something then he would help me just do it. Hearing his voice and discerning his will was what I needed to learn.

I still had a bunch of friends I loved to be with at church and school. I loved to laugh, hang out, play games, be silly, use all my accents, and act out scenes from movies; but, there was something changing in my world. It seemed like I was suppose to find my strength in being alone with God. I felt singled out. I could identify with the story of the eagle who flies solo much of the time and eventually must hide in the cleft of the rock only to pull out his own feathers so stronger feathers could grow and take him to higher heights.

69

Being set apart was necessary. God needed my undivided attention. I could no longer just blend in. I was on a journey with the Almighty. I had chosen to put him first, to fear him above all else, to yield my life and my will to his. I had answered the call, now came the consecration.

Consecration was my decision to dedicate my life to God's service. It came in the call and the yielding; and, now it would come in the daily surrender. Every day would be a choice. It came in big ways and small alike. It was the process of learning how to die to myself, to sit still, to wait and to worship, whether I felt like it or not. It was perfect in my youth. When you are young, unattached and available, you are free to abandon all else and follow. Daily devotion to a set goal brings purpose, focus, clarity, and meaning to your life. Devotion to God himself lines every other thing up. Life starts to make sense. Even the hard parts have meaning. It all works together for good. **It wasn't about getting it all right; it was about getting to God**. I had a lot to work out. I had a lot of dying to do. God was faithful. He gave me grace to change, to yield, and to allow myself to be corrected. I learned that God's discipline came from love. A father that loves his son corrects him.

I learned that everyone has a cross to carry, not to pay for their sins but to die to self – to say no to your own will in order to follow God's will. I had dreams, God dreams. He placed them in my heart. He gave me an imagination, a sense of adventure, a love for people and nations; but, I would need to learn how to hear God, to hear past my emotions, to follow by yielding to God's spirit. Timing would be everything. A good thing at the wrong time is not a good thing. So I made friends with Matthew 16:24-25 and let it light my path. "If anyone would come after me, he must deny himself and take up his cross and follow me. For whoever wants to save his life will lose it but whoever loses his life for me will find it."

The temptation when you're young is to feed your own flesh, to entertain yourself, fill up your time with "fun," make yourself feel good. Some of it can be a distraction and so very empty. Much of it leads to dead ends. Proverbs 14:12 says, "There is a way that seems right to a man but in the end it leads to death." We really don't know what is best for us a lot of the time. We need to rely on God.

I was learning to trust God. Anywhere he led me I would be able to grow and it would be used ultimately for my blessing. I didn't have the fear that if I gave God everything there would be nothing left of me. He was trying to make more of me, to help me discover myself, to be confident of who he made me to be. If I yielded myself completely, he wasn't going to ship me off somewhere and make me do something I didn't want to do for the rest of my life. It was quite the opposite. Psalms 84:11 says, "No good thing does he withhold from those whose walk is blameless." God wanted to bless me, to fulfill every dream that would be good for me. His dreams for me were actually bigger than mine and I had some biggies; but, in order to sustain a blessing there must be character. There must be a test. There must be a passing of the test to move forward. God was too kind to let me run ahead without preparation. He wanted to equip me. He wanted to set me up for the best. He wanted me to shine, to come forth as gold. I am so grateful for his patience.

Redemption is what Jesus did on the cross for me. Accepting his great sacrifice and believing in him was my first step. Once I believed and confessed my faith, the process of sanctification began. God was helping me by the power of the Holy Spirit to become more like him. There was a desire to do the right thing, a righteousness that comes through faith. I wanted to please God with my life. Then came the call. It seemed two-part: God was drawing me and I was asking the question: "Lord, do you want to use my life?" In my spirit it was clear he did. I had the passion and the vision but I was still missing a piece. Then came the test. I failed him miserably; but, this didn't change his call or his promises. Romans 11:29 says, "For God's gifts and his call are irrevocable." He would have kept pursuing me. And he did. The love came so abundantly and so undeservedly. It was hard to take. It all came to a crossroad. It was all or nothing. I responded again in consecration when I devoted my life to his services. This was the absolute marriage of all that is infinite and eternal to what is finite and mortal. Heaven and earth walking together, precious and perfect even in the midst of all my limitations, humanity, and a fallen world. I was back to the garden in my heart.

Pearl Power

Are you at a crossroad? Have you ever felt singled out? Do you wonder if God has a special plan for your life? If your answer is yes to any one of these questions this is a very good sign. You are conscious that God is working in your life. Don't talk yourself out of God's work in your heart. He cares deeply about your life and he has a wonderful plan. You haven't missed it. He's just too big to miss. Today is a great day to surrender it all.

Let The Games Begin!

I signed up for my first mission's trip and was heading to Venezuela. I was finally going to Latin America! I started practicing all my Spanish phrases and got a bilingual Bible. It was such a dream. I couldn't wait to finish up my junior year of high school just to take the trip. I had told everybody that I wanted to become a missionary and this was my first opportunity to see what it was really like. It was an adventure waiting to happen and I was ready! Just a month before the trip I received a call that it was canceled due to a revolution that had broken out. I felt like a popped balloon. The let down was awful. My youth pastor, Rich Catapano, had decided to take a mission's trip to Germany and asked if I could join him instead. I didn't speak a lick of German yet I knew God could use me anyway. I could sing! That always blessed people. Latin America would just have to wait. I would get there one day... just not this particular summer. Shucks!

I didn't realize signing up for Germany was really signing up for an intense three-week spiritual-warfare training trip. Germany, outstanding for all its beauty, brilliance, and rich cuisine, needed Jesus desperately. We were housed over a fabulous bakery, slept in down blankets, and ate the finest of food; but, each day we did not leave our meeting room until we were prayed up. We worshipped and prayed for four hours at a time. I didn't even know you could spend that much time with God a day! It was powerful! Our hearts were fully engaged with heaven. We learned so much from simply staying and waiting on God, never mind all the ministry opportunities that ensued. It was amazing! I learned a lot from Rich; namely, his teachings and his heart for the lost. He wanted to see people's lives changed, the church strengthened, and hearts transformed. And he did! It was a great start; and, it set me up to spend unlimited time like that with God when I returned home. Why not?!

I practiced everything I learned in Germany and found that spending time with God was quite addictive, in all the right ways. Besides, I was young and it helped keep me on the straight and narrow. Next came my senior year. I needed all the help I could get!

Spending time with God and journaling became a must. Every day was a miracle waiting to happen; but still, there were some days that stuck out more than others – days you marvel at how clearly you can hear his voice and how evident his will becomes. The oldest journal I could find was from January of 1988 – the last semester of my senior year of high school. My dad had begun to teach me about goals and dreams. He said it was good to start the year with a vision: where I see myself going, what I'd like to accomplish, and what I felt I was made for.

My Journal:
January 1, 1988 (17 years old, senior in high school)

Today is the first day of the rest of my life. It is the beginning of a new year and a brand new challenge in my life. As I look back on 1987, I see a lot of failures and defeats along with many beautiful experiences, triumphs, and victories. I pray the Lord will show me the way and guide me to do what He would like me to do!

My Goals for 1988

Grow Closer to the Lord

    —Prayer

    —Devotion

Learn to Read Music

Play Synthesizer (keyboard)

Sing with a Legitimate Voice

Find College with Major in Biblical Studies

Music & Drama

Liberal Arts

Mission's Trip

    —Spanish-speaking country

    —Finland

    —Germany

Teen Talent

Vocal Winner

Christian Band

That year I grew in my devotion and prayer life, became a better piano player and singer, was accepted to a great Bible College, went to Paraguay on a mission's trip, and won a music talent contest. Huh, there really was something to all this! Writing it down was part of seeing it, praying it, believing it, and becoming it. Pretty cool!

February 7, 1998

"Delight thyself in the Lord and he shall give thee the desires of thine heart." —Psalm 37:4

February 11, 1988

Thank you Jesus for your patience with me. Please give me the patience and understanding to deal with others and myself as you do.

February 14, 1988

Valentine's Day!
Christianity is not boring!
We have the power to do great things!

It was around this time that I decided to write a list of what I wanted in a husband. I realized that whatever I wrote about would need to be matched with my own character and growth. If he was all I hoped he would be, I needed to be the same for him. That was both a challenge and an inspiration! In any case, I needed to write it down even if by faith. I had prayed for him off and on for years now ever since I signed the paper with my dad when I was 12. It was good to get a vision of this awesome man of God. I would write a few more lists until I got it down pat. Some of my ideas were superficial at first but I kept writing until they made sense. Then I treasured that piece of paper, storing it in my Bible cover. I didn't realize at the time how precious all my writings would be and how important it is to write down your vision.

Pearl Power

Write your dreams down. Be specific. Think about where you want to be in a year or two. Write down your goals. Give yourself somewhere to aim. Don't limit your goals by your own resources. God has a hidden storehouse. Your job is just to dream, to write it down and to ask. God will help you discern what you should focus on. Be flexible. God is working it out. Write down anything you sense might be a God-idea. Don't get stuck in doubt. Just believe!

Decisions, Decisions

My Journal:
February 29, 1988

Dear Jesus,

Please confirm this college decision in my heart and in my spirit.

Please show me what you want me to do in ministry. I love you Jesus!

My dad and I took a wonderful trip to a Bible college in Pennsylvania. As soon as we stepped into the chapel we could feel God's presence. We both knew it was where I needed to be. Tears rolled down our cheeks as we raised our hands in praise. It was an easy fit. I knew I could seek God there and grow. I wanted my roots to go down deep in Christ. It was not a fancy place but it was full of God's presence. This was the most important thing to me. I could see myself being prepared there. It was not my first choice; but, when praying about God's will it's more about surrender than making your own dream come true. God knows best. His peace would make it clear where I should be. I was very grateful my dad was there to confirm. He gave his blessing and was just as excited as I was. Priceless!

I knew my father loved me. He told me all the time. He shared stories of when I was a baby and how I would hold his cheeks and say, "Daddy, you're just so cute." He would try to teach me how to pronounce the word *milk* correctly by saying, "Silk milk, skunk munk." I always responded with a smile and said, "Please pass the munk." He loved retelling the story about how I'd unexpectedly pull my cup out from under the pitcher while he was pouring. I simply had enough. He got a kick out of me. I thought he was cute.

As the years passed, I noticed we didn't relate as much. I had always talked to my mom about everything; but, it was at the end of high school that I came to find there was a longing to be closer to my dad. My heart needed his covering, his accountability, and his guidance. Deep down, I started to recognize the temptation to look for attention elsewhere if it was not found in a father figure. If I didn't work things out with my dad, I might end up trying to work it out through boyfriends or even husbands. After taking the trip to visit the college I decided to talk to him about it one day. It was awkward and I didn't know how to word it; but I mustered up the courage and asked if he would talk to me more, check in with me and see how I was doing. He seemed a bit caught off guard, and told me he was giving me all he had (or all he thought he had) and doing much more than his dad ever did. He reminded me that his dad never even said he loved him. I think he may have underestimated his ability to relate to me. He may have thought he didn't have what I needed or felt inadequate.

I understood what he was saying but felt very rejected. This didn't work for me. I was upset and disappointed. I figured since he was a dad and a Christian he should at least try. I didn't realize his inner struggle. I ran up to my room crying and told God how unfair this was.

The truth was that my dad was doing and being much more than he was ever shown. The fact that he was a praying man, faithful to his wife, plugged into church, accountable to his pastor, hard working and an amazing provider were all signs of character, strength and integrity. He had allowed the Lord to work in so many areas of his heart.

As I cried in my room, I felt God's comfort but soon after I also sensed he was saying very clearly that if I wanted a deeper relationship with my dad I would have to be the initiator. Huh? I reminded God about my justice button and how unfair that was, that he was the adult and I was the child. For a week I held my case with God but every time I brought it to him I got the same response: "If you want a relationship with your dad you need to initiate it." My assumption was that parents, particularly Christian ones, who know God and pray, should be the initiators of all family growth and forward movement in the home; but, the truth was that sometimes children need to lead up. Sometimes the child has been given opportunities and even teaching that the parent never had as a child. Instead the parent went through major challenges and didn't come to faith until their adult years. That's a big difference. It is a huge advantage to come to faith as a child. I had to humble myself, put my preconceived notions aside, drop my judgments and accept what God was saying. I would have to "be what I wanted to see". Finally, at the end of the week I laid it all down and was willing to "initiate".

It took some time. After a long day, dad would come home and sometimes take a plate of food to the den to sit and watch TV. I knew he was whipped and probably had emptied himself out at work but I was important too. I was determined to share my life with him. So, I planted myself right next to him just waiting for a moment. I felt a bit obvious but the longing to connect was greater than my pride. I was willing to put myself out on a limb. It took some time but eventually he switched the TV off and turned to me, asking how I was doing. That was all I needed. I smiled and gave him a piece of my day. It wasn't as hard as I thought. I would imagine he began to think the same thing. He had everything I needed. I wasn't looking for some nugget of wisdom or a pep talk. I just wanted him. I wanted to tell him what was in my heart and know he cared. With this we began to build a fresh, new start. It wasn't long before my college days began. I would be far away but Daddy wrote me notes. They were simple and sweet. That's all I needed!!!

Pearl Power

We need to be covered. God can provide that in many ways. He knows how fragile we are. He knows we need good, godly examples and leadership. Sometimes he provides that through our immediate family and sometimes he sends mentors. Your father may not know how to connect with you. He may not feel like he has what you need. You might have to be the one to initiate. But whatever the case, you can pray and ask God to bring the right covering. He will not fail you.

Can I stay now?

Taking the mission trip to Paraguay the summer after high school graduation was an absolute dream come true. Latin America felt like my second home. I couldn't believe how totally comfortable I was. I immediately fell in love with the people. It was all I had hoped for and so much more. I was actually so happy there I didn't want to come home. When I called my parents, my dad very graciously reminded me that Bible college was waiting and I didn't have his permission to stick around. That did the trick! The calling without the proper character and timing can lead to all kinds of problems. A good thing at the wrong time is just not a good thing. I still needed a lot of work. Proverbs 19:2 straightened me out with, "It is not good to have zeal without knowledge, nor to be hasty and miss the way." I had to grow and learn. So I stood on the promise, "He who began a good work in me will be faithful to complete it." I was still a minister in the making and one day I would return!

August 7, 1988 (summer missions trip to Paraguay)

We stopped in Panama, Ecuador, Peru, and Bolivia before getting to Asuncion, Paraguay! That means we were in six countries in one day! Well, the country is just what I expected it to be and I love it!

Today the missionaries told us they were taking a road trip once and one of the guys needed to use the restroom. It was in the middle of the night and they were on a dirt highway. There was nowhere to stop. So, they decided to stop on the side of the road in the pitch black. The fellow got out and made his way behind a bush. Suddenly a light came on. He was on someone's front lawn fairly close to their front door! Just then a few people walked out the front door to see what all the commotion was about. He hightailed it back to the bus! These missionaries are cool!

It is so much fun to see real people in real life situations in ministry being absolutely accessible. Real life on the mission field! I can do real!

Pearl Power

Have you ever taken a trip out of your town, city, state, or country? It really helps to get a broader vision of the world. We can get greater vision for our lives and future when we learn about other cultures and people groups. Ask God for opportunities to see your world and learn more about all the wonderful people.

Magazine Guy

Growing in God didn't mean everything would be smooth. There are some things in life we wish we could redo. We get in a situation and we cave; we don't get to say what we hoped we could. We have a running conversation in our head with a person we no longer see. They're long gone yet the fight hasn't stopped. You wish you could have said a few more things, maybe stood up for yourself, told them what you really thought. You come up with better responses, maybe something that sounds a little smarter than what actually happened. Then you realize once again it was never said and you have a heap of regret and a bunch of dead-end roads in your head.

One thing I know about God is that he doesn't leave us with dead ends. He will always give us other opportunities to stand up for ourselves – maybe not necessarily with that same person but with the same stuff: the fear, anxiety, loneliness, addiction, for example.

The summer after my senior year of high school, my friend Jeannie and I decided to go for a trip to New York City. We had been best friends since we were twelve; sharing a deep love for God as well as comedy. No one could make me laugh harder than Jeannie. Every girl needs a friend like this! Now we were on our way to the Big Apple. We had visited many times with our families, but never alone. We were excited! What an adventure coming from the suburbs! We drove down to her dad's job, parked there, and took the bus the rest of the way... big girls! Ha!

While walking along the street, this tall, handsome, young fellow befriended us. He was quite the flirt and even seemed to have a sparkle in his eye. We were young and easily flattered. He proceeded to share his "magazine business" with us and invited us to McDonald's to sit for a minute. After about 10 minutes of going through all his magazines, I told him I wasn't interested. He decided to work on Jeannie. I motioned to Jeannie for us to get going. The young man insisted that we buy something and that he needed the business. I could see Jeannie was uncomfortable but didn't quite know how to shake him; she was still feeling somewhat like Jell-O from all the compliments. I got up and said we had to go and then he turned. In an instant he went from nice to very naughty, even perverted.

He was now trying to intimidate us since his seduction tactics didn't work. As we got up from our seats he was now belittling us and trying to make us feel insignificant so he could tower over us. He was a scammer. There was no business. He just wanted cash. By now I had grabbed Jeannie's hand and began to run as he stomped after us cursing down the street. He kept coming with all his insults and oppression. It was nothing less than demonic. We finally lost him in a crowd but we were still shaking from the trauma. We had never seen anyone act this way. What seemed like an innocent connection turned into a nightmare. From start to finish all he wanted was to take advantage of us. None of it was truthful. We had walked into a big lie.

For years I yelled at him in my mind. I came up with some really good lines and tried them all out on him. There's a saying "Don't let people live rent free in your head." Man, he was taking up so much room and paying nothing. All I wanted was another chance to push back. I was mad at him for how he treated us; but, I was also mad at myself for letting him pull me in, subjecting myself to his flattery and intimidation. I knew it wasn't the guy I wanted to meet again but I desired a like-situation where I could make better choices, where I could just plain stick up for me!

A couple of years later I was studying at a Bible college in Pennsylvania, just outside Philadelphia. My friend Rachel and I decided to go to the King of Prussia Mall. It was the largest mall in America at that time. Woohoo! We weren't really there to buy anything. It was just nice to look around and get off campus for a minute.

It was a slow day at the mall. The main halls were pretty empty. We took a stroll by the fountains when all of a sudden this young man appeared. He had some magazines in his hand and started his spiel. I couldn't believe my eyes. There he was!!! We were hundreds of miles away from New York City and years had passed; but, I knew the face well! I had grown up a bit now and was ready. I smiled with wild surprise and said, "I know you!"
He quickly retorted, "No, no, no you don't." My eyes were crouching in on him like a cat ready to pounce on a mouse and I yelled "Yes, I do!"

I leaned over to Rachelle and whispered to her to get security. Her big brown Brazilian eyes grew wide. She was shocked and said, "What's going on?" I told her I would explain later and to just go get security. Then I got right up in his face and said, "You're not selling magazines. You're a scammer!" He jumped back and tried to deny it but I re-told my story in a loud defiant voice. I could see fear and anxiety flood his face as he could no longer compose himself. He yelled to an accomplice who had been hiding on the other side of an earring pagoda, "Dude, we gotta get out of here!" That's when all heaven broke loose on my behalf as I screamed, "Security!" My moment had come!!! Now the roles had reversed and I was chasing him!!! I was no longer afraid.

I never did catch that guy but I sure did catch that stupid spirit of intimidation. I put it under my feet. I was so free of that thing!!! Jesus gave me a second chance. I laughed all the way home, partly in disbelief and partly for the sheer drama! It was outrageous! My own reality show! Cinematic for sure! I loved chasing him. I loved screaming, "Security!" and I loved being free! Justice had prevailed in my world. Only God could know how much that meant to me, especially since he made me with such a huge justice button.

You know, every girl should have a "Security!" moment where she's sticking up for herself just because. One of these moments builds upon the next and she finds herself getting stronger from the inside out. It's the kind of confidence that gives her poise, self-esteem, a sense of personal value in her surroundings. From choosing off a menu to choosing a life partner, this kind of God-confidence will direct her to best-case scenarios. She's worth the effort! The world will be a better place because of her stand. She doesn't see herself as better than; she has greater compassion knowing what it took to make those choices for herself and she longs for others to know the same freedom. She is humbled by her transformation and knows it's a God-thing. She is a woman... Whoa Man! Ha! And God is all about giving her a second chance to show it.

> "For you have been my hope, O Sovereign Lord,
> my confidence since my youth."
> —Psalms 71:5

Pearl Power

God loves to give us second chances. Sometimes we need to ask for them. We should never feel less than others or let people make us feel insignificant. We are all to be respected as individuals. God-confidence gives us strength to stand up for ourselves. We choose with whom we will associate. Those who are disrespectful do not deserve our time or energy. Respect starts with our own heart. If we respect ourselves others will have to follow.

"A malicious man disguises himself with his lips, but in his heart he harbors deceit. Though his speech is charming, do not believe him." —Proverbs 26:24-25

SIX

To Be or Not To Be

"In his heart a man plans his course,
but the Lord determines his steps."
—Proverbs 16:9

Graduating from high school and moving off to Bible college was wonderful! I still remember the trip to the store with my mom to get all the college essentials: laundry basket, sheets, pillow, umbrella, detergent, hangers, cleaning products, pens, paper, and all this other stuff you think you need. It's nice to have some new things, a fresh start, and a fresh vision for life. It was happening. I was becoming!

I'll never forget my first night there. We had a freshman ice cream social. This must have been before we were told about all the rules because I was sent back to my room to get changed for wearing shorts. Okay, a little embarrassing but no biggie. I would be right back. It was free ice cream. I was moving ahead ready to gain my freshman five!

I loved college! I wasn't crazy about studying all the time. I wasn't really looking for a man, but I was crazy about my time with Jesus. I would kick myself out of bed in the morning to spend time with the Lord. Yep! Sometimes it came easier than others but I loved my time with God! The first part was always the hardest – getting my flesh to die. I had to get past myself to get to God. I would begin by worshipping the Lord, then reading the Bible, writing in my journal, praying, and then back to worship.

My Journal:
November 18, 1989

Dear Jesus,

Thank you for the time that I have with you this morning. You are so precious Lord. I want to know you. I want to walk with you, talk with you, and allow our relationship to grow. Thank you for blessing me in every area of my life. I know that I need you and that I cannot <u>really live</u> without you.

I pray that today I would use, exercise, and practice all that I can in what you've given me. I pray Lord that I will learn to take more risks and allow your grace to flood my life. I pray Lord God that I would learn to be much more studious. I want to learn and I want a passion to learn. I pray Lord that your peace would become more and more real within my life. I love you Lord! I pray that as

I go home for Thanksgiving I will be a light in my family, whether I recognize it or not. I pray Lord that I will not react out of my flesh but that I will be calm, peaceful, slow to speak, slow to anger, and quick to listen. Slow me down Jesus!

Lord I thank you for my job. Thank you for all the blessings, challenges, and growing experiences you have placed with it. Thank you Lord for meeting my needs.

I love you with all my heart! You are my God!

... and on and on the trickle became a stream and then the stream became a river, slowly and steadily until at some unknown moment I would sense God's wonderful presence fill my room and I would cry and worship and cry and worship and cry and worship – with a roll of toilet paper handy of course. Tissue boxes always ran out too quickly. I would stay as long as I could. Then off to classes, activities, study groups, laundry mats, and the cafeteria; yet, I would always find my way back again in the evening. On chapel days I would get there early and find a room nearby to worship the Lord. I would sing and pace about, praying for things, then maybe on my knees for a bit in God's presence and then off to chapel. I would be looking for any and every opportunity to be with God. It was very special. He was looking for me too.

On those days when I was running behind, maybe hit my snooze button too many times and was late, I could feel the loss. I had missed an opportunity. I would get a gentle nudge to head back to him... never guilt or shame or condemnation – that's not how he works. I would have a sense that he missed me just as much as I missed him. Pretty amazing considering he's the one keeping the earth on its axis, holding the planets in place and the sun at the precise distance. The same one who spoke the world into existence was longing for me... me! Ever patient, ever kind, always loving even when I would totally screw things up and get things wrong. God didn't run out on me; he never has.

I loved worshipping the Lord through music, anywhere, anytime. I had taken singing lessons growing up but I didn't learn to worship in my singing lessons. I learned to worship in private – whispers, melodies, words... sometimes soft, sometimes at the top of my lungs (depending on location and hour). I learned to sing scripture and pour my heart out in song to my God. What an amazing discovery! I was made for worship! I was always aware of worship at church, but this was different. I was now deciding to worship God by myself, on my own, initiating moments with my Savior. Powerful!

One journal started out with:

Dear Lord,

I thank you for being so real in my life. I thank you for greater convictions, for opening my eyes, for favor and for drawing me close. I want to be a sweet-smelling fragrance to you. Since my name means flower I would love to express that in my life to you.

Lord, I pray that your angels would camp around me. Please continue to purify me and build within me an undivided heart, singleness-of-mind, and the wisdom to obey you and do your will.

I believe that obedience is the greatest priority I need to fulfill in my life. I want to be obedient to you Lord. I thank you Lord that I can crucify my flesh, feed my spirit, and walk in the Spirit. Thank you for illuminating your word to me in James chapter one. I want to be what you want me to be.

A Few Days Later...

I'm in a mess Lord. Please help me out. Show me how to treat people properly. Cleanse my heart; forgive me for speaking right out of my sinful nature. Please show me how to humble myself, deny myself, and pick up my own cross. Please break every wicked way in me. I need you to wash over me and clean me out. Show me how to live for you.

Thank you for your loving kindness toward me even when I'm not so lovingly kind. Please help me run to you when I'm tired and lonely. I need you to fill my emptiness and give me strength. Please forgive me for trying to do everything out of my own strength.

Draw me closer! Thank you for your conviction. Thank you for grabbing a hold of my heart. Feel free to grab it every day and help me get rid of this pride! Show me how to be an example, how to forgive and not get an attitude. I need your help Lord. You are so good. Thank you for giving me so many opportunities to sing and share with the youth. I leave my life in your hands!

My writings remind me of Paul the Apostle when he said, "I do what I don't want to do and what I should do I don't do." Life got messy at times. I complicated things. Some days I got it right and some I didn't. I was just a work-in-progress. He loved me the same. Crazy grace! It's pretty humbling. His mercies would come rolling in new and fresh every single morning. Faithful indeed!

Life is like math. You learn one part and it builds on the next. If you don't quite get it, you go back and learn it until you can build on it. I was never crazy about math; but, I can see how God was using all the details of my life to help me grow. The good, the bad, and the ugly – it all works together.

Pearl Power

Jesus is the most stable part of life. Everything else can be shaken and a lot of it will but Jesus is solid. He will never be shaken. He's the rock beneath all the other moving pieces. Taking time with him sets the tone of the day. Steady.

Julio Ricardo Rivera Sanchez

One day, during my first semester of college, I made a declaration in chapel during prayer at the altar. I must have been pretty loud because some of my guy friends quoted me on it later. I cried out to God stating that I would give him five years of my life. "FIVE years Lord!" I was emphatic. How I came up with that timeframe I cannot tell you. I must have been having a moment. It all had to do with singleness. I was laying it down. I'm pretty sure God was cracking up. Not just because he knew what I was about to do but because of how long it would actually take to get married. You give God a time constraint and he might just double the time.

Not long after, I was visiting my family on a weekend and met Julio Ricardo Rivera Sanchez. He was a handsome evangelist from Columbia who had a passion for God like I had never seen. I instantly became inspired to learn Spanish! I was conversational at the time but became very willing to expand my vocabulary. I bought a bilingual Bible and this was how we talked. Julio would preach around the tri-state area. So, on the weekends I would join him singing and praying and speaking as much Spanish as possible. It wasn't long before we were dating and my five-year plan was out the window. I admired Julio for many reasons. He taught me how to fast and pray, to chase after God, push into his presence, and wait for God. I watched him follow the Lord and it inspired me. Lots of people who knew my heart for missions and his passion for ministry saw it as a God-thing. It seemed to make sense. We ministered very well together and enjoyed seeing people get saved and set free.

After a year of dating Julio we decided to go to my dad to ask for the blessing. My father had put a silent fleece before the Lord (basically he asked for a specific sign). He didn't have the green light, so he told us to wait and keep praying. I wanted to get married but wouldn't think of it without his blessing. And then of course, there was the little paper I signed with my Dad as a twelve year old. I hadn't forgotten. I was so glad I had done that so many years previous. It made such an impression on me and really helped me when life started to unfold. So we waited.

Pearl Power

Waiting is an option. It's not impossible. Sometimes we can't see the whole picture until we wait a bit. Then we're glad we didn't run ahead. There's great wisdom in waiting. It can protect us.

A Day of Decision

A few months later my family had planned a trip to St. Lucia. I was invited but I really didn't want to go. After praying, I was compelled to take the trip. All the way to the airport I had a funny feeling about things and I began to pray under my breath. I prayed all the way to St. Lucia. As we were about to land, the pilot said that the aircraft before us had been swept off the landing strip and we had to return to New York because the weather was so dangerous. I believe God had me on that trip simply to pray. When we returned to New York I felt released from the trip. I had done my part so I went to visit Julio. When I shared with him what God did it sent us into worship and prayer. While praying, I felt compelled to speak with one of the girls from his youth group. I sought her out and shared what God had put on my heart. It came down to a very strong word that this was a day of decision. I explained to her that I was supposed to be on a trip with my family that very same day and how God sent me just to pray because of the danger that was ahead. I felt the same way about her and her situation. She had to choose at that moment whether or not she would trust God and hand over her life. She began to cry and told me that she had plans to go to a hotel with her boyfriend that night. I was amazed at the severity of her situation. I begged her to turn around but in the end she gave into the boyfriend. That night she got pregnant. Her life would never be the same.

Pearl Power

God is not someone to toy with. That day made me realize how important it is to follow God's leading and to do what he asks, even when we don't quite understand or feel like it. Life is precious and there are critical moments to pay attention to. The Bible says today is the day of decision. Choose this day to lay down your life. Don't wait until tomorrow. It's not guaranteed.

My Italian Connection

One gloomy, rainy day I was at the laundry mat in town when I noticed a pregnant lady trying to fit on a bicycle with her two children and laundry. This was a sight to behold! I introduced myself and asked if I could help. The older son, who was just six, spoke happily for his mother. They were an Italian family; the mother did not speak English. For some odd reason, I took Italian my last year of high school and knew just enough to connect. Isn't God good! The rest was hand signals and translations from the little boy. I loaded their laundry into the front trunk of my '73 Super Beatle, got the children settled in the little backseat, and strapped the bicycle to the top. The sweet little mommy smiled in gratitude and we were on our way. They lived a couple of miles down the road, right above a pizzeria. We laughed at the way everything worked out as we made our way to their home. At our arrival, I met the father who was making pizza downstairs. He was a bit more serious and his English was limited; but, he was grateful and welcoming. I stayed a minute for some seriously strong espresso, the kind that puts hair on your chest. We shared as much as we could for a first visit. This would be just the beginning of many talks.

I made a point to check on them once every couple of weeks. The children always came running. There was typically a lot of loud talking, strong espresso, and laughing. Sometimes the mother was quiet at first, but then she always loosened up by the end of our visit. Looking back, I'm sure they were trying to make ends meet most of the time, as life for them was hard just starting out here in the States. There was a lot I didn't understand and could not relate to, but I kept visiting. One week I got them an Italian New Testament. They loved it. A few months later I had found an evangelical church that had an Italian service in Philadelphia. They agreed to go! So, we all packed into my Beatle once again and traveled 30 minutes to the church. I didn't understand very much of what the pastor was saying, but they sure did. I could see their eyes were wide and they were really paying attention. At the end of the service there was an altar call and they all stood up. Actually, the mother stood up and made the rest of them stand with her. She was a small woman but certainly a force to be reckoned with. I loved this little family. They were a gift and a treasure.

Pearl Power

Our lives are strategic. God uses every part. Sometimes we can't see the purpose until years later. Our willingness to let God use it all increases our opportunities.

The Bank and the Bug

Another time I was in the bank in town when I heard some commotion coming from the parking lot. I looked out to find that a little old lady had actually parked her car so close to mine that she connected the two by the left corner panel of my '73 Super Beetle. We needed to get a tow truck to disconnect the cars and then my car needed to be fixed and repainted. She was so embarrassed but I kept telling her everything was okay and it would get taken care of. Insurance paid for it all. It looked brand new in just a couple of weeks. I took her information and asked if I could visit her. She looked at me in disbelief and said, "Sure." I would go visit her with some popsicles every few weeks. At first she didn't quite trust me. I could see she was wondering what my deal was, but then she realized I was just being friendly. She was precious. I loved hearing her stories. She made me miss my adopted grandparents, the Paneths, who lived next door to me when I was growing up. They were from Hungary, a wonderful couple who loved us dearly. We always had the best conversations. Old people have amazing stories. You simply have to sit still long enough to let them share. Now I was older and appreciated the conversations even more. This little old lady had some wonderfully inspiring stories. It was a gift and a warm welcome in the midst of my studies!

Pearl Power

Ask an older person to tell their childhood stories. Just sit and listen. It may take some patience and discipline to hold steady but you will be amazed at how much you enjoy what you hear and how much you can grow from their life. You need to hear and they need to tell.

Angel for a Day

One of my favorite things to do at college was to get prayed up in my room and then head over to the local hospital to pray for others. I would walk right to the elevator, hit whatever button looked appealing and then spend a couple of hours going from room to room, quietly asking if anyone needed prayer. I was never refused. It was more of a covert operation – undercover intercession. I liked to go in the evenings, just before dark. People need hope in dark times. It amazed me how many people didn't have family or a friend to visit. It was sweet and sad at the same time. Some needed to share their story. I would listen and pray what God put on my heart. I knew praying was the most important part. That's what would change everything. The Bible says our prayers are "powerful and effective." I didn't need to be eloquent. I simply needed to ask. There was always a smile or a *thank you* in return and then sometimes tears and a big hug. Some of the patients even asked if I was an angel. A few times I made it around to the ICU. No one ever questioned me, so I would pray quietly and make my rounds. It's amazing how many opportunities there are to reach out to others all around us. It just takes *a grain* of faith, *a teaspoon* of spontaneity, and a half *a cup* of willingness. Most of what I did came down to my own willingness. God would always come through with the rest. He really is tons of fun!

Pearl Power

Pray and ask God to use your life in some amazing way today. Look for opportunities to pray with people. Yes, even strangers. You'll never know how much fun it is until you try it. Be brave! And when God does something amazing give him the credit. Tell someone!

What Can You Do?

"Whatever your hand finds to do, do it with all your might." Ecclesiastes 9:10

While at college I held a few different jobs. For a season I cleaned the bathrooms. I loved the acoustics. You can have fun singing in a fully tiled bathroom. I think I actually got in trouble for singing too loud. Then I moved on to a cleaning company off campus. I loved cleaning this one apartment because the mother was a working single mom with three children in tow. She needed some TLC. The apartment always looked like a total wreck; but, that made my purpose all the more clear. I would do extra just so she'd feel loved and taken care of. The mom frequently complimented my work and eventually told the cleaning company. She added that I did more than the other cleaning ladies. I think I got fired for cleaning up too much. I took too long and did more than they wanted. Funny how that works sometimes; but, it was all part of "growing!"

During the summers I had interesting jobs. One year I was a house mom for troubled teens. There were seven girls from the ages of 13-17. Each of them had pretty intense stories. I was glad to bring peace and joy to the home. Some of it was tricky because I had to take them to doctor appointments and tell them about certain sexually transmitted diseases that some of them had contracted. I cried with them and prayed with them when possible. There was a lot of anger and a lot of pain. Sometimes you get a window into someone else's life and it makes you see how much we all need Jesus. Only he can fix the world.

Another summer I worked in a big sister program with a girl who had mental challenges. I would take her to the park, out for ice cream, read to her and just be a friend. She was a teenager and a very precious person. The idea was to simply get her out of the house. Sometimes everything was smooth and sometimes she would get upset. When I prayed it seemed to make her more upset, even if I was praying under my breath. I decided to pray before going and that worked out better. There seemed to be some confusion in the home. Something was not right but it was not my job to fix it or to judge the situation. I was there to love and to pray. It was a window into her life. God wanted me to see some things and to have compassion. This was part of the journey with him, doing "whatever my hand found to do."

Think Free

I love free stuff. Once I was in a CVS (a local drugstore) with a friend. She needed to get something so I went in with her. I looked around, found some lipstick I liked, and went up to pay for it. When the cashier scanned it, the register read, "Gift for you." She scanned it at least five more times but every time it came up the same, "Gift for you." She got frustrated and called the manager who came up and scanned it as well. The two of them stood there dumbfounded. Finally the manager put it in a bag and said, "Well, there you have it. It's a gift for you!" I was pretty amazed – so was my friend. She kept saying, "You didn't pay ANYTHING?" "Nope," I said.

There's one thing that is kind of hard to get our heads around at times. It's called forgiveness. The truth is we could never pay for it; but, because Jesus died for us and paid for our sins we can be forgiven and we can forgive. It's a *Gift for You*. Forgiveness truly is underrated. Yes, it can take some time to work through, especially when you need to grieve and heal, but there's nothing like being free! If you take even the smallest step in that direction, God will meet you where you are, no matter how far you have to go. You just need to think FREE!

Freedom and forgiveness became a huge issue for me at Bible college. There was a day when my world fell apart. I had been studying to go into full-time ministry, loving

Jesus and loving people. I had poured myself into ministry on the weekends, made my room a haven for girls to come and talk, ran after God with my whole heart, seeking him in prayer and worship. But unfortunately I had also found myself in a verbally abusive relationship by someone who lived in close proximity. I think I actually took pride in sticking around even though the person treated me like garbage; I was holding on to the "turn the other cheek" concept. In most cases I would have held my personal respect line and moved away from the situation; yet, somehow I seemed to carry a false sense of responsibility to help this person change.

There were plenty of red flags. The verbal abuse went on for over a year and a half until one day, out of the blue, the person flipped out over a minor incident. She busted down a door, threw me into a bathtub and started pummeling me. I yelled for her to stop and threatened her with calling the police. Finally I managed to get myself up and ran to the Dean's office with wet hair and bare feet. I told them what happened and was asked to wait. I waited for 45 minutes. They called the girl in but she had another story. I was still in shock and really speechless at how no one was taking care of the situation. I decided to call my dad. After I explained my situation he asked if there was a helicopter pad on campus. He wasn't kidding. They didn't have a helicopter pad; so, he told me he would call the police. A little while later, I saw a sheriff's car pull up in front of the window to the school but I wasn't allowed to talk to him. They hushed the whole thing and sent him away. I was told to carry on with my day. What? I was still shaking and now I was nauseous. I made my way back to my room in disbelief and utter humiliation. I was studying to be a missionary. I wanted to help change the world. What was all this?

The drive from my hometown was at least 3 1/2 hours. My dad was there in 2 hours and 25 minutes. He was obviously driving with the pedal to the metal. He had canceled all his patients for the day and ran out the door to rescue me. He would usually see between 85-125 patients a day at his clinic, sometimes as many as 160. I knew this was a huge sacrifice, but I needed him more than ever. Dad was my hero. I got into his car and finally calmed down.

I was still kind of numb about the whole thing for the next few days. It seemed like a living nightmare; but, I kept talking to God about it. I was honest about how I felt and needed to verbalize how wrong this was. I felt like he agreed with me. The situation was awful; Dad affirmed me but he also gave me my only real option right from the start – forgiveness. If I wanted to be free from the situation and not carry it the rest of my life I would need to forgive. I told him I wanted to and started to ask for help. I had a feeling this would be a process. I was committed to letting God work the wrong things out and the right things in; yet, I still had to grieve in order to start my healing.

When I returned to school I found that my things had been junked in another room. The tears welled up as I opened the new room door to find my things strewn everywhere. Immediately I heard the Lord say, "There is a choice here. You are not powerless. You can get bitter or you can get better?" "Help," I cried.

Later that week I received a letter in my mailbox which stated that I was on probation because I had been involved in the situation. It was a shocker to say the least. I was now being punished for getting beat up. I remember thinking, "How on earth does this stuff happen?" If it were only the injury and even the part of being denied my rights at the Dean's Office I could have moved through a little quicker; but, the shame that ensued was enough to throw me over a cliff. The enemy is so cruel. It's very typical of an abusive situation for the person attacked to feel shameful for being involved. It doesn't make sense but it's what we feel. Even having to tell someone what happened feels shameful. I had learned Psalms 34:5 when I first started singing at church to help with my nervousness. It says, "Those who look to him are radiant; their faces are never covered with shame." I knew that was the truth and decided to hold onto it and let it take a deeper root in my heart.

Once again I could hear the Lord speaking to me. "The enemy is trying to sift you." This is what Jesus told Peter. The enemy was not just trying to give me a hard time. He wanted to take me out. He was looking to get a hook in my heart that would keep me in a dark place. Was I responsible for all this? No. But I was responsible for how I would handle it. Only I could choose.

As I walked down the path to my dorm with the probation paper in my hand, I ran into our missionary in residence, a good, godly man. I told him what had happened and he just said, "Fiona, God is sovereign. He can use this." He had spent many years in India and saw a lot of injustice. I had to land on God's sovereignty. He was still in control even though my world looked out of control.

This was a lot to take; but, the truth was that I was not going into ministry because of a certain school or church. I knew I was called by God himself. I started ministering as soon as I sensed that God wanted to use my life when I was a teenager. I had a bright future before me with dreams and promises. Yes, the enemy wanted to snuff me out. He was looking to kill, steal, and destroy every area of my life, but mostly my faith. This was not simply injustice it was a full on attack against my life and my future. My battle was not so much with that person but with the enemy. I knew if I held my peace and kept my eyes on Jesus he would deliver me.

I started to be able to say, "I forgive" and fill in the name. I had to forgive the main person but then I had to forgive the school leaders who put me on probation and even the people who junked my stuff. When bad thoughts came I would say out loud, "I forgive." I literally had to say it hundreds of times a day in order to move past all the hurt. My heart had been broken. Freedom has a price. To fully grab hold of all Jesus did for me and release those people I had to work through some layers. Someone told me that when you don't release people you are letting them live rent free in your head. That made a lot of sense to me and it motivated me to forgive them. I sure didn't want them hanging around in my head of all places.

One day I heard the Lord say it was time to bless them. I thought, "Wait a minute, forgiving was one thing, blessing was another." Then the Lord explained that when I could bless them I would know that I was truly free.

It was true. Months later I found myself, by the grace of God, being able to bless them. It floored me how free I felt. It was a different kind of freedom, something I had never experienced before. I found myself blessing them all the time just because it felt so good. For a couple of years I carried this tradition. I learned later that *a curse undeserved cannot rest and neither can a blessing.* If the person is not worthy of the blessing it comes back. I'm not sure how all that works but I may have been blessing myself for a few years, only God knows... Ha!

You, my friend, have the same Jesus with the same power to forgive and release others from living rent free in your head. Think Free!

My Journal (at that time):
March 23, 1990

Psalm 23

Even though - it doesn't matter - if I walk through the darkest valley. Not run but walk, taking it slow. Through, not around, not above, but right through the valley of the shadow of death; the worst, almost fatal, and the darkest, where I cannot see a thing. I cannot see the mountain. I cannot see the vision or its peak. I don't know what the future holds.

I will walk and I will not fear evil. I will not fear death, nor demons, nor tragedy, nor Satan. No evil. Nothing evil! Because JESUS is with me!

Your rod and your staff, they comfort me.
The rod is for protection and the staff is for discipline, to pull me back in line.
The Comforter is the Holy Spirit.
He will not allow me to be overtaken but will give me guidance and direction.

Pearl Power

There is nothing too difficult for God to heal in your life. He wants you free. Forgiveness is a gift from Jesus. We can receive it and we can give it because of what Jesus did for us. It starts with your willingness not your feelings. God will meet you in your surrender, he will give you grace for this and he will heal your heart. You do not have to carry this for the rest of your life. Think Free!

The Stuff God Uses

In my free time I loved visiting people who needed a pick-me-up. When I was home from college I would make time to visit a couple of old ladies from the church named Mary and Greta. They were in their 90s by the time I was in my 20s and they now lived in a nursing home. Getting a visitor was a big deal. It made their day. They had given their lives to ministry, never married, and always had smiles and hugs to share. It was a pleasure! Shortly after the hardship I experienced at Bible college I decided to pay them a visit. On my way out that day, Mary handed me an anonymous article called "God Uses Things That Are Broken." I have to share...

"God uses most for his glory, those people and things which are perfectly broken. The sacrifices He accepts are broken and contrite hearts. It was through the breaking down of Jacob's natural strength at Peniel that got him where God could clothe him with spiritual power. It was breaking the surface of the rock at Horeb by the stroke of Moses' rod that it let out the cool waters to thirsty people.

109

It was when the three hundred elect soldiers under Gideon broke their pitchers, a type of breaking themselves, that the hidden lights shone forth to the consternation of their adversaries. It was when the poor widow broke the seal of the little pot of oil, and poured it forth, that God multiplied it to pay her debts and supply means of support.

It was when Esther risked her life and broke through the rigid etiquette of a heathen court that she obtained favor to rescue her people from death. It was when Jesus took the five loaves and broke them, that the food was multiplied in the very act of breaking, sufficient to feed five thousand. It was when Mary broke her beautiful alabaster box, rendering it henceforth useless, that the pent-up perfume filled the whole house. It was when Jesus allowed his precious body to be broken to pieces by thorns and nails and spear, that His inner life was poured out, like a crystal ocean for thirsty sinners to drink and live.

It is when a beautiful grain of corn is broken up in the earth by death, that its inner heart sprouts forth and bears hundreds of other grains. And this on and on, through all history, and all biography, and all vegetation, and all spiritual life, God must have BROKEN THINGS.

Those who are broken in wealth, and broken in self will, and broken in their ambitions, and broken in their beautiful ideas, and broken in worldly reputation, and broken in their affections, and broken oft-times in health, and those who are despised and seem utterly helpless and forlorn, the Holy Ghost is seizing upon, and using for God's glory. It is "the lame who take the prey." Isaiah tells us. It is the weak that overcome the devil. God is waiting to take hold of our failures and nothingness and shine through them.

'Because the foolishness of God is wiser than men; and the weakness of God is stronger than men.' I Corinthians 1:25"

This article changed my life. I realized this was one of my common threads, brokenness. It was exactly what God would use and must have in order to fulfill his purpose. Any moment I felt broken I could hand it over to God and let him use it. After all, God uses things that are broken.

My Journal:
November 11, 1990

Thank you for helping me through this day, for showing me my weaknesses and where I need to grow. Oh God, I know that I need you now more than ever. Jesus, please move in me. Have your own way in my life. I love you Lord and I need you! Help me open my eyes, ears, heart, and hands to you. I want to serve you with all my mind, heart, and strength. You have called me. You will equip me. I am nothing without you Jesus! Be blessed and glorified in my life!

Your Servant, Fiona

Pearl Power

God wants to take your broken pieces and make something really magnificent. It doesn't seem possible but it really is. Just like the Bible says, he makes beauty from ashes. It is a process and God is committed to helping us through. Humility says "Take the pieces and make something pretty." This is God's favorite thing to do. He is our redeemer, making all things new.

SEVEN

Up, Up and Away

"Make level paths for your feet and
take only ways that are firm."
—Proverbs 4:26

My Journal (2:30 am):

Teach me Lord to look ahead at future effects of my actions and show me how to choose the right direction no matter how much more difficult your way is. And please multiply my sleep.

The last couple of months at Bible college were challenging. I was still working through the healing process. I started to realize there was more to ministry than just getting a four-year degree, marrying Julio, and heading to the nations with a certain church. I had boxed things up pretty tight. It seemed that there were quite a few others at the school who questioned their own situation as well. They longed to be used by God but limited him to "the ministry." We started to discuss what we actually loved to do. One girl had a dream of becoming a National Geographic photographer. She had talent. I encouraged her to follow the dream and do it for Jesus. Another wanted to become a nurse but felt conflicted. I told her to do both. Be that nurse everyone needs, that will minister to body, mind, and spirit. Another wanted to teach in public schools. I told them God put the desires in their hearts. They were free to serve him in any capacity. Recognizing what you actually love, being honest about your dreams, and being prepared was the key. This made me wonder about my own situation. I had a call but God could do any number of things with me. I began to investigate. I wanted to be prepared for anything. I came to the same conclusion. God was moving me on.

I moved back home and signed up for community college. As I settled into my new college surroundings, I found that God could use me just about anywhere. Ministry was my life. I became the first woman president of the Spanish club, the first redhead and the first gringa to join. How fun! I even continued to minister on the weekends at churches in the area with Julio, all the while holding down a job.

By this time Julio and I had gone to my dad twice for the blessing and each time he said to wait. I didn't understand it. We had prayed, even fasted for a whole week before asking the second time. It had been two years; but, my dad, with tears in his eyes, said he didn't have a green light from God and that we should wait. Before going into that conversation I found the scripture, "I can change the heart of the king like I can change the course of a river." I knew God was the one directing the show. He would tell my dad when or if. It was hard to take, but I was resolved to get married only with the blessing of my father. I knew it was my protection even if I didn't understand the *whys*. God was sovereign. He controlled my destiny. I wanted his will. I trusted him.

It was at the end of three years of dating Julio when things started to shift. I was grateful for his friendship, our ministry times, his teachings on fasting and his example of seeking God; but, it seemed like change was in the air. I took a trip with my family to Florida and while I was there I decided to call Julio and ask for a couple of weeks to separate and seek God. I was surprised by his quick acknowledgment of the need to separate. It seemed like he had a heads up. After a few weeks it was obvious to me that God was saying *let go*. I was amazed at the grace to change directions once I understood it wasn't God's will. Especially because so many people were convinced we would get married. I remember explaining what I felt as I sat down at the Four Brothers Restaurant in Mahopac with my dad. He understood me perfectly because he didn't have peace to move forward. We called Julio and asked if we could all meet together. My parents prayed over him and we all cried together as we let go. It was like we all grieved the death of something and at the same time had peace that this was God. Not your typical break up situation, I must say, but truly God led.

A few months later, Julio confided in me that there was a missionary to Africa who had passed by his church on a Saturday evening. Her car broke down right in front of his church. She was still a long way from her speaking engagement that evening and because they were in the same denomination they called ahead to the other church to explain her situation, asking if she could stay and minister at Julio's church instead. The other church agreed and so she stayed and ministered. After the service, Julio went to her for prayer. He explained that we wanted to get engaged and had gone to my dad twice now. She stopped him and said, "This is not to be." He quickly explained how we had been ministering together and how much of a blessing it had been. She stopped him again and said, "Let me just pray." While she prayed, Julio began to cry because he could sense God was truly leading her words. When she finished praying she said, "In one month from today, Fiona will call you and you will separate. It will be hard but in three months you will both be emotionally settled. Do not treat her any differently this month. Do not tell her about this conversation until it has all come to pass. You do not have the same calling and she is not for you." It was exactly 30 days from when she had spoken those words to him that I called Julio from Florida. I was in awe of God. His timing is impeccable.

As Julio spoke about the missionary I started to recall a missionary woman that had visited me in Bible college during my last few weeks there. I asked if she was a beautiful single African American woman, from New York City, in her early 40s, with long dreads and a huge smile. He said *yes*.

This woman had come to minister at the college I attended back in Pennsylvania. I was so amazed by her life and passion for God that I befriended her. She invited me and a couple of other girls to her room to talk as she packed her things to leave. She was a mighty woman of God, brave and beautiful in every way. She told me God had great plans for my life and not to settle. I agreed and promised to stay the course. And now here I was getting complete coverage on the back-story and absolutely amazed by God.

It was about this time my father also explained his silent fleece that had kept me from getting the blessing. Julio had been in the process of getting his green card. My father had said to the Lord that if Julio got his green card it would be a green light and I could marry him. He had all the right paper work, a great lawyer, church support, endorsements, and financial backing but in the three years we dated it was a closed door. We didn't understand. Three months after we broke up his green card and all his papers showed up. God was working in all the details. Sovereign indeed!

Pearl Power

Life changes. Sometimes we think we've got things figured out and then it all gets turned around. It's really okay. God didn't miss anything. He will use it all. Our job is to stay in faith even when it's not what we hoped for. God will make things clear in his timing as we keep trusting him. Being flexible is crucial to following. The course might change a little but we'll get to the right destination. Trust!

Comfort vs. Calling

After accumulating a number of degrees at the community college I began wavering about doing mission's work. I loved ministry and was fully engaged in the Northeast; but, the call to the nations now seemed vague. I had been removed for a long time; and, truthfully, I had become comfortable. More than ever, I realized the sacrifice. I was already conversational in Spanish and was involved in many Spanish ministries; so, surely that would suffice, I thought. Besides, I loved my family and it would be much easier to stick around home. I was still waiting for HIM. HE hadn't presented himself yet. I wasn't planning on going without him; but, I could not deny this *longing for more*. I was not content. I knew I would need to chase after God to find out what came next.

Sometimes God is sneaky. He knows how difficult it is for us to make the right decisions when we can't see ahead; so, he puts out a carrot and we keep moving forward. One day I saw a flyer for a foreign exchange program to Quito, Ecuador.

It was a three-month program. I figured that was easy enough. Only three months. I can handle that! Something inside said, "Go for it." So I did!

My Journal:
January 2, 1992

What an awesome day! I am truly blessed. There is so much to be thankful for. I left the house at 5:30am with both of my parents. They saw me off at the airport (La Guardia). The flight was just perfect. The Lord gave me such clarity of mind. This alone was a miracle, considering I only had 3 ½ hours of sleep. I did rest slightly from New York to Florida, but I really slept from Miami to Quito. I had a whole row to myself. The Lord also provided very kind young men to carry my bags wherever I went (for free). I met a couple going to Quito who are world travelers. They were a lot of fun to talk to.

Finally I got through customs and saw two girls at the end of the walkway. The little one

(Gabriela) was sitting on the gate holding a sign that one of her brothers had made. It said FIONA DE LA MERE. I caught eyes with her and began to wave. The two of them immediately smiled and then their two brothers came around the bend as well. What a beautiful family! They all introduced themselves, shook my hand, and brought me to the car with a million questions. They are so great!

As we got to the car Mr. Rivas called out my name, opened his arms and gave me a Big hug. We all talked a mile a minute on the way home. When we got to their house (It's very nice.) I met Mrs. Rivas. What a love! She reminds me of Tante Irma (my adopted Columbian Aunt I had growing up).

The boys dragged my luggage up the stairs. I mean dragged! I cautioned them and then suggested that we might need to call my dad (the chiroprac-

*tor) for their backs when this is all over. Every-
thing is too good to be true!*

After arriving, I found out that the university I was attending was the top in the nation. All the diplomats, gov-
ernment officials, and people of influence sent their children to this school. Even the president's grandchildren attended. This was a bit of a surprise since I was sent by my
community college. I never imagined meeting so many
people of influence. I made friends easily as I had no personal barriers. I could be friends with the homeless just as
easily as with the wealthy. One thing I knew for sure is that
all people like to laugh and everyone responds to kindness.
And, of course, everyone needs Jesus.

The hardest part of the semester was getting the work
done. I was taking five courses in Spanish and each one had
its own vocabulary. But I managed to get a 3.8, which was
nothing short of the miraculous.

My daily conversations were always sprinkled with what
God had been doing in my heart. It flowed naturally out of
the time I spent with him, journaling, reading my devotional book *My Utmost for His Highest*, and getting scripture in
my heart and not just my head. There was always room to
grow. God made sure of that! Whatever I was growing in I
would share. It seemed that quite a few of my friends at college yearned to hear more, so we would get together after
school and talk about God.

I shared my faith in Jesus every chance I had, sang
whenever I could, connected with missionaries, and got to
church. A month after starting the program I was asked to
become an English teacher at the university. Among several
degrees I attained back home, I also received a certificate

for teaching ESL (English as a Second Language). I loved teaching and really enjoyed being called Profesora Fiona. **The world had truly become my oyster!**

Pearl Power

The world is a beautiful place. We shouldn't be afraid of new places, people or things just because they're different. God's glory is revealed through each culture, language, and people group. It is to our benefit, growth and blessing when we embrace the nations. We are all an expression of God's love.

The Old Lady with the Sticks

"Each one should test his own actions. Then he can take pride in himself, without comparing himself to someone else, for each one should carry his own load."
—Galatians 6:4-5

While I was a foreign exchange student, I would take the bus in the afternoons to my home in the section of town called Jipijapa (pronounced Hippie Hoppa, too much fun!). My street name was Jeronimo Leiton. I loved that too. It all sounded like an adventure! The hill going up to my street was very steep. Almost every day I would see this little old lady carrying a huge bundle of sticks up the hill. She must have been at least 70 years old. This was crazy to watch. I couldn't imagine why she didn't have any help. Wrapped around her shoulders and waist, she had a large piece of material surrounding the sticks. She was hunched over and it looked like it was painful. Sometimes I saw her at the bottom of the street and sometimes I would see her half way up. It was at least 10-15 blocks to the top.

One day I couldn't take it any longer. If she could carry this load I certainly could, that and more. I was strong. I had to do something. I jumped out of the bus early with my backpack and ran over to her. I said, "Good afternoon" and asked if I could help. She looked at me like I was joking and kept walking. I noticed that she didn't speak very much Spanish. She must have spoken Quichua, the indigenous language. I showed her my idea. I pointed at her load and then pointed at my back. I told her in Quichua, "Titu amitu Bendiciachi" (God bless you). It was one of the only things I could say. She smiled and stopped. I explained again that I wanted to carry her load and pointed up the hill. She started laughing. I just kept pointing to her load and then bent over and pointed to my back and then the hill. She laughed again and started to take the bundle off her back. It was quite an ordeal to get this thing off.

By now there were onlookers, watching quite attentively. Here was this tall redheaded gringa getting ready to put a load of sticks on her back. I was so excited and proud. I started thinking what a great testimony this was. That's right, we should help one another. We should carry one another's loads. No grandma left behind! Why just wait on the sidelines... get involved; jump in. Be somebody's hero... just like ME! There were sermons and life messages just pouring out.

As it was time to place the load on my back I noticed we would need a little extra help to get it up and on. I called someone out of the audience to participate, nothing wrong with that, right? This young man came over very willingly and helped place the load on my back. I was a bit surprised at the actual weight; but, I knew I was a strong girl and couldn't imagine this little old lady carrying something I couldn't carry. I was having a little difficulty breathing but figured that would go away when I pulled myself up and headed up the hill. I had now fastened that material around my lower back and around my shoulders to my chest. Everything was a go.

I tried to slightly pull myself up but couldn't. I tried to take a step but could hardly move my legs. I think the little old lady had been carrying close to 150 pounds on her back, if not more. I tried again, and again, and again... and nothing. Now I understood the hunching over part. This is when I noticed the little old lady in tears because she was laughing so hard. Her hair braids were swinging over her head as she keeled over cracking up. I laughed too. It was truly the only thing I *could* do. Yes, it was funny and quite embarrassing at the same time.

Most of the people started walking away realizing the show was over. No gringa hero today folks. Ay ya yai ya yai!!!! I think they felt bad for me. They really had high hopes. All I could do was say I was so sorry and that I couldn't move. I needed a couple of extra people to take it off this time. The little old lady was very gracious. She picked it right up again and started up the hill. "At least I provided some entertainment," I thought. I would never again underestimate the power of any little old lady.

Pearl Power

Everyone has their own load to carry. You have grace for what is yours. You will not have grace for everyone else's stuff. You'll just get stuck. It's best to carry your own load and bless other people along the way with encouragement and inspiration.

Mom and Dad Delamere   "Granda" My Mom's Dad

The Delamere Clan   Mom's home in Ireland

Best Friends Growing Up
Jeannie Left & Kathleen Right   Journals

L: Covenant with Dad
R: Husband List

Return from Colombian "Red Zone" Trip, Recording in Miami,
Rivas Family (Study Abroad Program) on the Equator

Giant Beetle in the Amazon, Mary and I in Paraguay, the woman
in the tower in Colombia

Youth Group in Ecuador, Verbo Mañosca Church, Ecuador

Elliot Speaks

Over 1,200 women gathered in the Bowman Gymnasium on November 2 to hear Elisabeth Elliot speak on "The Hope of Glory" as part of Nyack College's annual Women's Seminar. Not even the persistent rain could dampen the spirit growing inside the gym as the day began. There was a hub of activity as women registered, found their seats, and shared in fellowship over cups of coffee. After enthusiastic singing of hymns and choruses, a hush fell over the crowd as Mrs. Elliot rose to speak.

Elizabeth Elliot at Nyack College

Jim and Mary DeGolyer

"The Birdcages" in Mexico, Singing at Nyack College Homecoming

Michael and I — "Just Friends" in NYC, Pat and AnnMarie Mercadante

Michael picking me up for Billy Joel's Party, Original Invitation,
and Billy's House (Mike Roca, *Daily News*)

May 20, 2000

Mellett Clan
with Grandma
and Copper,
our dog

Michael and I ministering at Lakewood Church, Houston, Texas

EIGHT

I Will Not Be Bought

"Fear of man will prove to be a snare,
but whoever trusts in the Lord is kept safe."
—Proverbs 29:25 NIV

While I was a foreign exchange student I made friends with the people who owned the corner store on our street. I would pop in after school to get my chocolate fix. The precious family I lived with didn't always have dessert after dinner. I found that dessert was a very important part of my life. I made it a priority. Ha! The people who owned the shop were wonderful. It didn't take but a few conversations to find out that they were believers. So, I invited myself to their church and found that it was a lot like my church back home. It made it easy to jump right in, worship the Lord freely and receive the Word.

My studies were a big challenge considering I was taking five courses in Spanish (Ecuadorean Art, Ecuadorean History, Ecuadorean Literature, etc.) and I had just begun learning the language a few years earlier. I carried a big thick dictionary around the first two weeks and had a constant headache. Nonetheless, I attended church every Sunday and went to their home group meeting during the week when I could. It was good to have the accountability. I needed it.

I made friends with some missionaries (Pat & Ann Marie Mercadante) in New York just the week before heading down to Ecuador for this program. I was asked to sing at a missions banquet at a nearby church. They were the main speakers. You'll never guess where they were headed? Quito, Ecuador of course. Pretty amazing. During the three months that I was studying, I had the opportunity to connect with them. They loved to laugh just as much as I did and we always had a great time together.

When my university program was coming to a close, Pat and Ann Marie invited me to visit their church and elementary school. I had an immediate connection with the people and the place. They asked me to pray about becoming an English teacher for the last few months of the school year and offered me room and board at their home. I had great peace. Sometimes when you pray about something you kind of already know the answer; but, I think it blesses God to acknowledge him and thank him for what he's about to do. I accepted and I looked forward to the move.

On my last Sunday at the old church, I thanked the pastor for the time I had been there and told him how the Lord had opened some new doors for me. He assumed I would just head back to New York after my studies. I explained I would be teaching at a school and I would be living with some missionary friends during the last three months of my visa. He seemed a bit surprised and told me I could work at their church. I told him I had prayed about it and had peace. He then asked me to wait a minute and went to talk to the other pastors and elders. Three minutes later there were six men standing in front of me insisting that I work for their church. They told me they would pay me well. I relayed the previous information and told them I was grateful for the offer but that I had already accepted at the other school. They asked me to wait another minute. They regrouped.

When they returned they offered me an apartment, and a good salary. I was now surprised at how they thought I might change my mind with their generosity. But by this time I started to feel disrespected. They weren't listening to me. When I did not accept the second time they decided to reconvene. This time when they returned the men surrounded me in a circle and spoke forcefully. They said they would provide a car, an apartment, a good salary and that I *would* take the position.

I was not to be bought. I explained emphatically that I had prayed, developed a relationship with these people at the other church, and that I had peace. The peace alone would tell me where I should be. I was not looking for opportunity I was seeking the will of God and I would not be persuaded otherwise. They were *not* happy and stomped around in disbelief. I didn't know if they were more thrown by the fact that I wouldn't take their impressive offer or that I was just a woman who would not succumb to the intimidation. I was not afraid of them. I would not be bought. I would not be manipulated. I was answering to God, not man. The best thing I could do was just leave, and that I did quite promptly.

Pearl Power

The fear of man is a snare. It will limit how much you are willing to follow God as opposed to man. When you know you have heard from God, when you have his peace and when you are making choices that are Spirit-led you can walk in confidence. And when all is said and done, the truth is, in the end you will only have to give an account to God, not man. Besides, obedience brings blessing and protection. Only God can see what's up the road. He has your best interests at heart. "The fear of God is the beginning of knowledge" —Proverbs 1:7. Putting God first is the smartest thing you can do!

Settling In

Living with Ann Marie and Pat Mercadante was a real privilege and pleasure. Their love for God and people was tangible. It was a huge bonus that they came from a town right by where I was born and raised in New York. It gave me a great sense of peace and familiarity among all the cultural adjustments. Pat and Ann Marie were of Italian decent. They spoke English but also threw out a lot of Italian words. Sometimes they mixed a little in with their Spanish. Gracias, Grazie... Sure! Close enough! I thought it was just great. We laughed a lot. They treated me like a daughter and covered me as I was maturing. I'm pretty sure they even covered quite a few of my blind spots in the process. I adored them. Every evening when we would sit for dinner I could feel the steam climbing up my face from my hot plate of food. That was before we started to pray. Oh, these two could pray! By the time we had prayed around the world my food was usually lukewarm. The first few times it happened I was a bit miffed, longing to fill my belly after a long day of work; but, then I grabbed hold of the absolute treasure of these moments. I began engaging and prayed my boldest, biggest prayers along with them. By the time we had traveled the world in intercession I experienced a whole new level of gratitude and fulfillment.

We lived on the side of Pichincha Mountain, which had a volcano in one of its peaks. The forest leading up the mountain had lots of interesting critters. There were big black scorpions that would come through the fireplace into the house (The darker the color the more venomous). One morning I met a big five-inch fellow outside the front door on my way to teach. His tail was lifted ready to strike. I grabbed a pole and gave him a good smash. "Out of my way! I am a woman on a mission! I don't have time for fear." And off I went.

When I told my parents about all the opportunities the Lord was opening up in Ecuador they were very supportive and gave me their blessing. They had traveled to Ecuador for their 25th wedding anniversary a few years previous and were familiar with many of the missionaries; and yet, they still wanted to make sure all was well with me. So the day before my birthday my dad called and asked what I would be doing to celebrate. I told him it would be a pretty typical day, nothing too exciting. He said, "What do you think about me visiting?"

"Tomorrow??!"

"Yes. Is that okay?"

"Sure! I would love that! Can you do that? Oh, please come!"

"Well, I'll call you if it works out."

"OK?!"

My father is one of the most planned out individuals I know. For him to come meant he was closing his office and had to let go of many obligations. This was no small feat for a self-employed doctor; but, I was on his radar and he wanted to make sure I was okay. What a dad!

I had this funny feeling he would actually come. In the middle of the night I woke up and started to pray for him. I looked at my clock. It was 3am on the dot. What I didn't know was that Dad had prayed and asked the Lord to wake him up at 4:00am if he was to go to the airport. My 3:00am prayer time was his 4:00am wake up call, as there is a one-hour time difference. He woke up, took it as a sign, and headed to the airport! It was my 23rd birthday!

I was proud to introduce him to all my new friends and church family. He was so proud of all God had been doing through me. Our time was precious! This was such a wonderful gift. It was redemptive, as you remember, my father and I didn't always have a very close relationship.

One extremely important part of our relationship was his covering. I stayed under his spiritual umbrella. I would ask for his blessing in everything I did; and, not only ask for covering but I also steered clear of things he did not feel comfortable with. I trusted my dad's wisdom and discernment. He, on the other hand, would pray great bold prayers for my life and hold me out loosely before the Lord, knowing I belonged to Jesus. And then track me down in other countries if necessary! I can't imagine how hard that was for him or my mom but they trusted God! Trust goes a long way.

We rented a jeep and I took him around Quito and some of the nearby Indian villages. We had a blast! As a token of the trip and our time together, he bought me a beautiful pearl ring. The pearl spoke volumes to me as I treasured my daddy-daughter time. I felt very affirmed. This let me know I was on the right track in following God and it meant the world to me!

Pearl Power

God will affirm your steps as you yield to him. Being accountable to your parents or those he has entrusted you to, trusting their covering and allowing them that place of influence in your life will prove to be a safe guard. If you need accountability or a mentor, ask God. He will provide just what you need. He can even send someone from another country to affirm your steps if need be. He is God; all powerful, all knowing, always loving and ever interceding for you. He is able.

The Galapagos Islands

Dad's trip was a total success! Now it was Mom's turn! My introductory story in chapter one of a trip to Colombia came just before my mother's visit. Mom is a missionary at heart. She loves the nations and celebrates all cultures and people groups. She has always made a point of embracing as many other people as possible. Her friends are a collage of nations. When she was growing up in Ireland it amazed her to see people from other countries visit, as they came few and far between. She shared this love with her children, a delightful pleasure in gaining friends and gathering a greater understanding of culture. No fear of differences, rather the absolute joy in celebrating them. She is intrigued with how people communicate, how they share humor, what they eat, and how they process life. It was never a surprise to find her in the kitchen perfecting a Vietnamese soup, Persian salad, Italian chicken dish, or any variety of international desserts. We call it the dance. She loves to try new things and does it in a way that draws you in and makes you want to try it too.

This time Mom was visiting Ecuador with the Galapagos Islands in mind. She had done her research and knew it was a must. Bucket list and beyond! My sister Siobhan, a very willing companion, joined her and we were off on my spring break to experience what these islands had to offer. Six hundred miles off the coast of Ecuador we flew into a small airport and boarded a yacht. The first evening on board there was open seating for dinner. So, we split up. After dinner my mother called me over and asked if I recognized a man at her table. I was surprised at the strong resemblance he had to the first friend I had made at the university and told them so. The man responded that he was indeed my friend's father, an Ambassador from Africa. We became immediate friends. From that moment on he insisted that the chauffeur pick me up at least once a week so I could join his family for lunch. He didn't have to twist my arm!

On our way back to Quito he called me over to his bench in the airport. He was a warm and gentle man; yet, he carried great stature – both physically and socially. He made you want to sit up straight, put your shoulders back, and your chin up. Placing his great big arm behind me in a fatherly way, he confided that he needed wisdom in how to handle his son, my friend. Since his wife's sudden death a few years previous, their relationship had grown cold and conflicted. He told how he had taken away privileges and laid down rules but that there was a lack of respect and obedience. He was obviously frustrated. All of a sudden I realized the ambassador was asking *me* for counsel. I started to pray in the spirit under my breath; and, then the words came. "Before you can establish rules you need to secure the relationship. Affirm him as your son. Let him know you love him. If you pursue him as a person he will know it's not just about the rules but that you truly care – rules without relationship is a perfect setup for rebellion. Yes, he needs to respect you, but it sounds like he is still grieving the loss of your wife. He needs *you* now."

I sat amazed by the words that were coming out of my mouth. It made a lot of sense. I was learning as I was speaking. He then turned to me and said, "You are very wise for your years. Thank you for your counsel. I will do as you said."

I smiled and thanked him for his trust and let him know what a fine young man his son was. It was a God-moment. I marveled at the conversation for weeks. Wisdom from above is powerful! The Bible says to ask for wisdom and God will give it liberally, meaning a whole bunch. Surely, there was an "abundance" that day.

Pearl Power

You can ask for wisdom and you should. Only God knows what is going on behind the scenes of each life. We can trust God to give us what we need in any given situation, conversation or struggle. All we need to do is ask. He can even fill our minds with the right thoughts and our mouths with the right words. He wants to help. He loves to bless us with wisdom. Just ask.

My 93 Year Old Angel

After my student visa expired I was invited to return to Quito, after a summer break in the States, as a full-time missionary with the church. I had mixed feelings. I loved teaching at the university. All the students were heading into their careers and they appreciated every little bit of help they could receive; but, teaching preschool through 8th grade was a different story. It was one of the hardest jobs I ever had. By the time I was heading home for summer break I wasn't sure if I wanted to go back to do that same hard thing for another whole year. But the truth was I was seeking God for his will not mine, and no matter what my feelings were I would not have peace until I relinquished my will and was willing to do whatever God wanted. Before leaving, I ran into Jim DeGolyer, one of the head missionaries. He asked me a simple question.

"So Fiona, what do you like to do?"

"I'm sorry. Do you mean what do I think God wants me to do?"

"No. Just what do you *like* to do?"

Hmm, I had never been asked that question before. I was always just trying to figure out God's *will*, what he liked for me to do, where I should serve, and what kind of work needed to be done. Sometimes I had even felt like all my dreams had to take a backseat in order to lay down my life and pick up what God was asking me to do. The truth was I liked singing and leading worship but that didn't seem to be an option.

He insisted, "Isn't there something you love doing?"

"Well, yes, I love to sing, to lead worship."

"Oh, that's great. I'm sure the Lord will use your singing." He smiled a big Jim-smile and off he went. I had been helping out on the worship team and any other opportunity given. Sometimes when I was praying for people, I would get a little song and just sing it over them. It was more than just a gift, it was a passion and a delight.

I repeated the conversation with the Lord and reminded him of how much I wanted to sing. My dream was to lead worship anywhere and everywhere. I loved mentoring young girls, leading the youth, praying with people, visiting them in their homes, and serving in just about any other capacity, but leading worship was tops.

Yes, I also loved the kids at the school and all the wonderful people. I just didn't like the paper work. So lame, I know! I prayed, earnestly asking God what to do and he spoke to my heart very simply and said, "Teach." He told me that he would work on my character through teaching. Well that seemed to make matters worse. I knew it would be hard; but, to add working on my character sounded like I was in for it. Yikes! This was not the adventure I was looking for. So I wrestled with God throughout the summer until I was all out of peace and miserable. Finally I agreed a couple of weeks before school started. Of course, all the peace returned. I sure do like peace!

I called my missionary friends, Pat and Ann Marie to let them know I would be coming and told them I would call back with my arrival information. The only problem was that they now lived 30 minutes outside the city in an area that lost power every couple of weeks. Sometimes it would be out for two weeks straight. Every time I called back, there was no answer. They didn't know what day or time I was to arrive and I was getting in at 10:00pm. By this time, everything would be basically shut down. There were taxis but it would cost an arm and a leg to get that far, and you couldn't really trust one to go that distance with a young woman by herself. I knew God had a plan and I was trusting him. I just didn't know how he would work it all out. So I simply boarded the plane in New York and tried to call again in Miami on my layover. No answer. I didn't want to make my parents nervous so I didn't tell them that little detail about getting into a foreign country at night, with no one to pick me up and nowhere to stay. Besides, God had gotten me into this, he would get me out. I tried to call a few more times and then got on the plane to Quito, Ecuador. I had this amazing confidence that things would work out. I was being obedient and I knew that God would bless me. That's the way he works. There was this tremendous sense-of-expectation and even a deep-seated joy, a silly little giggle manifested a knowing of his will.

In first class, I had a window seat in the first row; it was comfortable. I looked out at my dear country one last time and thanked God for how he had already worked this situation out. He had gone before me. He had a plan. I would find out His plan when I needed to.

As I rested my head back, I could feel a little old lady next to me looking toward me. I turned to her and smiled. She pulled out a little booklet and started to share about Jesus. It had lots of sweet illustrations about believing, repenting, and crossing the bridge to God through Jesus. I just let her share and went along with the whole thing. She was doing so well I didn't want to interrupt. At the end of the booklet it asked some questions: Where are you? Did you cross the bridge? Do you know Jesus as your Savior? I was so happy to tell her I had crossed the bridge. She was delighted to find out that I was a believer and also to realize that I could actually speak Spanish. So many people would look at me and assume I could only speak English.

We spoke about the Lord for a long while. It helped pass the time. She told me she was 93 and had known the Lord almost a century. I was blessed to have her as my flying companion. Just as we were about to land she asked who was coming to pick me up. I told her I wasn't exactly sure. She said she had five sons and at least a couple of them would come for her. She said she could have one of them take me home, if I needed a ride. I thought that was very kind; but, I wondered if their car would be big enough for my American-sized suitcases and where I should go considering it was so late.

Sure enough three of her sons came. They were probably in their late 60s. One of them had a pickup truck. That was a good sign. At least my suitcases would fit. I had peace as the little 93 year old lady hugged me and blessed me. Off I went with God's miraculous provision. As we pulled out of the parking lot, the man asked, "Which way should we go?" I thought to myself, "I can't go all the way out of the city with this guy. It would be much too far. Maybe I can go to Jim

and Mary DeGolyer's home?" I had been to these missionaries' home once before. It was a three-story apartment
building surrounded by a sea of three-story apartment
buildings and I had seen it during the day. How on earth
would I find it now? At night? In a city of 300,000 people?

I felt a familiar nudge. It was the Holy Spirit. "Turn left!"
I couldn't tell the man exactly where we were going because
I didn't know; but, I just kept telling him, "I'll know it when
I see it" and gave him the little nudges I sensed in my spirit.
Left, left, right, left. We were now at least five miles from the
airport. I felt so confident we were heading in the right direction. It was kind of crazy! As we headed down this one
street I sensed we were supposed to make a right but it said
One Way (Una Via) – we would be going the wrong way. I
told him I was sorry but I really thought we should go down
this street the wrong way. It was late and dark. There was no
one around, so he agreed. Lord only knows what he must
have been thinking! I didn't have a street name or number
or anything!

As we made our way down the street, I started to look
up at the buildings and then all of a sudden I said, "Stop.
Here we are!" All I can say is things looked "slightly" familiar
but I couldn't really be sure until I saw Jim & Mary's faces.
By now it was close to 10:30 pm and these folks liked to go
to bed early. I rang the doorbell below and waited at the
gate. I was truly amazed at how much peace I had. Not a
drop of fear. Then, they appeared at the second story window with three of their children laughing in disbelief.
"Fiona?!"

When I explained it all we just sat in awe of God. He is
awesome! They told me I could stay in their maid's quarters
that night. It was small, but perfect. Before I made my way to
my room, Jim said, "I'm so glad you've come back Fiona. We

are just about to record our first international worship album and we wanted to know if you would like to sing on it?

As if God hadn't done enough. I just started to cry in amazement that this was all part of the big plan. When I said *yes* to God about returning, I wasn't just saying *yes* to teaching but also to many recordings and ministry opportunities throughout Latin America. The teaching position did afford me many character-building moments; but, it also held my job at the church while I traveled with the church's worship band and international worship ministry. There was a lot to this whole "yes" thing – more than I could ask or think or imagine.

Pearl Power

It's always the little doors of obedience that open to the palaces. I've found that any time God has tested me to trust and obey, he always had much more in store than what I thought I was sacrificing. You can never out give God! Obedience brings blessings!

NINE

Favor Like a Shield

"For surely, O Lord, you bless the righteous;
you surround them with your favor as with a shield."
—Psalm 5:12

Originally I was supposed to live outside the city of Quito at the Mercadantes' home, but when I arrived that night at Jim and Mary's, things began to shift. They could sense it was going to be a long trip each day into town and decided to offer me the room I had been staying in. I appreciated their kindness and accepted. I had no idea how much this would bless my life.

Remember God loves little spaces to work with. This was one of those precious nooks in the world where God revealed himself daily. I had a bed, a shelf, a closet, and a little step up to a sink, a toilet and a shower, all within reach. The room was across an open patio on the top of the three-story building. I had a key to go out the patio door and then one for my room. The space on the patio was perfect for gathering a good group of girls and sharing God's wonders under the star-filled sky of the Andes. There was also a ladder attached to the building that went up to the flat roof. That was just for Jesus and me.

I marveled at God's provision. My home was in his heart. His will gave me the greatest sense of peace and satisfaction. This is the joy of a surrendered life. Nothing else compares.

Jim and Mary also lived this life, completely surrendered and willing to grow with every new season of raising their beautiful family. They had traveled from California to Guatemala with a group of young people hungry for God and eager to help the world. It was a rescue mission to help restore Guatemala after a horrendous earthquake took the lives of more than 30,000 people in the 1970s. While they were there, taking care of the needs of the people, they began to share God's love. They started a Bible study and met in homes until it became evident God was calling them to stay in Latin America. Eventually the church grew throughout Central America and down into South America where Jim and Mary were planted.

Jim was always on the cutting edge of spiritual growth and anticipated new books to help his family as well as the ministry. He loved to see people get set free and receive inner healing. He was a passionate visionary. Mary was the balance, a perfect compliment to all his strength and vigor. She was strong too, but her strength came from her peace. As a mother of four, living in a foreign country and embracing the life of ministry, her family was her very first priority. Her marriage and children came way before any other considerations. I respected that.

Jim would challenge me with deep heart-questions and caused me to think outside the box. Mary would make simple statements like, "If you can read, you can cook." It was liberating!

I was always amazed that they could be in total disagreement and not lose their cool. It was okay not to agree on everything. It was okay to have different opinions and to respect each other as such. They built each other up even in their disagreements. They were *one*. I was impressed!

This atmosphere was a great place for me to grow and heal. I actually didn't realize how much I needed it.

As a leader, I helped facilitate a 12 Step Program. I don't think I even got to Step 2, when I realized I needed the program just as much as everyone else in my group. So I went through it with them. It was very eye opening!

This was healthy. I wasn't in ministry because I had arrived. I was in ministry because Jesus had arrived and he was committed to my wholeness. There were many moments in that year when I recognized how much I needed these people, all of them. I would pour out what I had and I would be receiving at the same time. It was a mutual blessing.

Pearl Power

There are times when God wants to do deep heart-work in us. He is waiting patiently until we get to a certain maturity to handle it. We can trust him to surface what needs to be dealt with rather than looking on our own for our flaws and hurt. If the Holy Spirit is dealing with us on a particular issue he will always make a way out. Even when we feel disciplined, he will never use guilt or condemnation. He will only use perfect conviction, which may show us the error of our ways; but, his conviction also, and always, edifies and comforts as it corrects. God will never lead us to a wall. There is always a window out.

Pennies with Purpose

I loved the school I taught at in Ecuador. It was called Verbo Mañosca, located right in the heart of the capital city of Quito. The teachers were very kind to me and the children were absolutely precious. I think they could sense when I was homesick and needed a little extra love. I would sit by them at their desks and correct their work sometimes. There were many moments when I could feel them playing with my hair behind my back or they would just snuggle up a little closer than usual. I got a lot of hugs! I think that's what kept me going. I loved and was very loved. At recess time I would run out in my long skirts and boots to play soccer with the boys or dance in circles with the little girls. Their joy filled my heart day after day. I really enjoyed them. Yes, God was working on my character as he promised; but, it wasn't as bad as I thought it was going to be. There would always be room to grow in life. This school made me feel very special and right at home, even in the midst of my maturing. Oh, the patience. What a gift.

One morning I was making my way to school and realized that this same lady was asking me for money day after day. She was sitting there with a child on her lap, in the same spot, at the same time, waving her hand at me. I got aggravated with her neediness and began to feel a bit of disdain in my heart as I sized up her situation in my head. All of a sudden, I heard the Holy Spirit very clear, "Really?! Really Fiona? You can't put an extra penny in your pocket for this lady. A penny?! Have you made me so small that I can't meet anyone else's needs but your own?" Immediately I lined up. God was right. The currency was at such a rate that we were only talking pennies here. One penny would make a difference in this woman's life. After that I made it a point to keep a bunch of pennies in my pocket whenever I was out. I was blessed to be a blessing, even with my pennies.

Pearl Power

God will not run out of strength to help us. If we are relying on Him we will have what we need. It doesn't take much. Just being available for God's love to flow through us can bless a multitude of people daily. Like those pennies with great purpose, God's love never fails.

The Bag Lady

One very normal school day I had just finished teaching six classes of English and I was whipped. The more work I gave the kids, the more I had to do. I was starting to catch on! I had a huge backpack loaded with homework and tests to grade. As I got off the bus and started walking down the block to my house, I noticed a lady going through the garbage. She was middle aged and kind of hunched over.

I stopped and asked if she needed anything and she said she was looking for bags, plastic bags. She explained that she could get money for recycling. I ran to find some in the house and when I returned I went to give them to her but noticed one of her hands was withered. I asked what the problem was and she said it just didn't work. Then I told her that I knew a very good doctor that could fix it. She said she didn't have the money but I told her this one was free. She looked up at me smiling and asked if I was a Christian. I nodded *yes* with a big grin and asked if I could pray for her. She agreed. It was a short prayer, simple and to the point: "Jesus, this lady needs her hand to work. Would you please heal it?"

All of a sudden she stretched out her hand and started swinging her arm around and around like a little kid. I was just as surprised as she was! We held hands and danced in a little circle, laughing and crying. It was just too much fun!

Then I remembered a little box of Tic Tacs I had in my pocket. I pulled them out and told her to take one a day and praise God for her healing. It sounded like a good prescription to me! She laughed and agreed. That was the last I saw of her. She probably got right to work after that!

Pearl Power

Miracles are a prayer away. You won't know how close you are to the miracle unless you ask for one. They come at unexpected times and in very unassuming ways. Jesus put dirt in the blind man's eyes. God doesn't fit in any of our "all figured out" boxes. He wants our faith to leap out in spontaneity. You don't plan a miracle, you just ask for one!

Just For Fun, Huh?

I had many close friends in Quito. Not all of them were Christians. The African Ambassador's family was Muslim. His three children were like family to me since we were around the same age and loved to talk, laugh, and eat. Their mother had passed away a few years earlier in a car crash and they were still learning to live without her. I took it upon myself to make them laugh any chance I had. "A cheerful heart is good medicine." —Proverbs 17:22

We would take day trips together and explore the countryside. I loved our conversations because we were so different yet carried such strong beliefs and convictions. I slept over their house once and even taught them how to make s'mores in their enormous living room fireplace. It wasn't exactly like back home in upstate New York where we would make a fire in the wheelbarrow in the backyard, sharpen some tree branches, and pull out a bag of marshmallows, a bar of chocolate and a box of graham crackers. There was a butler holding a silver platter of large pink marshmallows, silver skewers, fancy European chocolate, and butter cookies; but, I wasn't complaining. It sure did taste good!

One evening I was asked to join them for a special dinner party. They sent the chauffeur to pick me up. It was always a hoot to know I was living in the maid's quarters and serving as a missionary all the while having these extravagant opportunities. All I can say is, *God really has a great sense of humor*!

A long flowy skirt, blouse with brooch, silk scarf, high boots, bouncy red curls pulled back off my face, a touch of sparkly mocha eye shadow, shiny peach lips, pink cheeks, a bit of brownish/black mascara and I was good to go!

I felt honored to join them as there were many important people from the city attending. I was comfortable in just about any social setting. Actually I found it quite amusing at times by all the pomp and circumstance that some carried. You sure can make a big deal out of yourself.

This particular evening there was a beautiful and prominent newscaster attending. After dinner we gathered in one of the three large living rooms. She was sitting on the couch next to one of the ambassador's children when I noticed her picking up his hand to read his palm. I was slightly thrown off course and wondered if I should get up and walk out. I prayed silently and asked God what to do.

The ambassador laughed at what she was saying and said I should be next. I immediately said, "No" quite emphatically. He looked at me with surprise and said it was just for fun. I knew the danger and with that took the liberty to say it was not a game, it was crossing a line spiritually, and that I would not even consider taking part. To me that was being "treacherous without excuse". I had definite lines drawn in my mind about what the truth was concerning palm reading. I also knew I could trust God to give me a heads up on any pertinent information I needed for my life. If God wanted me to know something he would tell me. This was dabbling with demons and I was all too aware. My spirit felt very disturbed.

Again the ambassador stated that it was *just for fun*, trying to settle any uneasiness in the room. As he convinced the group by voicing his take on palm reading, the woman grabbed hold of his son's hand and said that he would marry an American. "No!" he stated in disbelief. She said it again and this time he yelled "No, that's impossible" with case closed, period, end of discussion in his voice. At that moment I piped up once again and said "Just for fun, huh?!" looking the ambassador in the eyes. This was no joke and we all knew it. Immediately the conversation turned and I became the object of scorn and ridicule. Some of them took turns hurling offense-ridden questions at me about my faith and my religion. I answered a few quite authoritatively and then all of a sudden heard the Holy Spirit say, "That's enough Fiona." This was not a battle of flesh and blood. I was not supposed to join the argument. I could be quiet. Let God speak for himself.

Needless to say I was not offered the chauffeur to take me home that night. But, interestingly enough, I was offered a ride by the newscaster. She seemed a bit chagrined as we entered the car in the garage. We were quiet making our way down the dark city streets and then she said, "You were right." I looked at her dumbfounded and said, "Then why did you do it?" She fumbled with her words and finally said, "I did the wrong thing. I'm sorry." I realized this was basically adult peer pressure. She was trying to fit in and do something that looked kind of cool – a bold move, but not a brave one. **Bold can do anything; brave goes after the right thing, even if it's a risk and the people you admire are not exactly admiring you back for it.**

My heart was broken. I really loved this family. I had been praying for them. When they would take their prayer break in their rooms during the day, I would be praying in the living room that they would see Jesus. I knew that God was working in their hearts and I would pray that he would reveal himself to them. At the same time, I was far from my own family, and they had made me feel so loved and appreciated. This was a great loss. I cried for some time before going to bed and then finally laid it all at Jesus' feet. Only the Lord could help now.

When I woke up the next day I still carried the disappointment. My heart was heavy but I kept bringing it back to Jesus. Then, around mid morning, the phone rang. It was the ambassador's daughter. She said they wanted to meet me in the park. I agreed and they said they would send the chauffeur. That was a good sign.

They were waiting for me. The daughter said we should walk together. She was a couple of years older than I, very dear, always smiling and sensitive, but carried great character. I loved her heart. She gave me a hug and we began our walk. Turning her head to me she said, "Do you know why we like you so much?" I quickly responded, "My red hair?" She said, "Yes, and..." slowing down a bit she added, "We know you walk with God." I was amazed and responded,

"Then why do you want to change me?" She smiled, "We don't." God was working all along.

Pearl Power

This situation with palm reading reminded me of a verse I had read in Psalm 25:3. "No one whose hope is in you will ever be put to shame, but they will be put to shame who are treacherous without excuse." Making a poor choice in the midst of your knowledge of the truth is a treacherous place to walk. There is no safety net. You're an easy target. Truth frees and preserves us from potential bondage. That's pearl girl power for you!!!

Jingle

I was hanging out one day by myself in Jim & Mary's home. I came down stairs to get something to drink when the phone rang. Sometimes I wouldn't hear the phone ring at all because my room was disconnected from the rest of the house. I had to go outside, cross a patio, and walk through a hallway to the office to get to the first available phone. It was enough of a miracle that I happened to be home and in the right place to hear it ring; but, when I answered the phone and they asked for me I was doubly surprised. This very nice lady explained that she was contracting a Coke jingle for the World Cup and asked if I would sing it. I told her I felt very honored and I would ask my agent. She responded very professionally saying, "Of course, of course. Can we call your agent?" I told her it wasn't necessary and asked if she could call me back in five minutes. She was thrilled, "Of course!" I hung up and prayed, "Lord, do you want me to do this?" He already knew about the money and notoriety I would get. I didn't need to explain anything; and, there it was, I knew exactly what he was saying.

The phone rang exactly five minutes later. The lady joyfully asked again, "So, can you sing for us?!!" I told her, "I am so sorry but it's not for me." The lady was shocked. She said, "We'll pay you very well." I told her again that it wasn't for me. She asked who my agent was. I told her God. Then there was this amazing silence on the other end. "God?" she repeated. I answered, "Yes, I ask him about everything." "Well, if you change your mind here is our number." And that was the end of that.

I told Jim and Mary about it later. Jim was amazed that I said *no;* but, the truth is that I never saw my voice as something to be used for just any kind of singing. I felt with all my heart that God had given me a gift so that I could sing with his anointing and touch people's hearts. I felt that my voice was something precious to be cherished and protected. The jingle simply wasn't for me.

Pearl Power

I can see now how God protected me. There could have been a lot of other temptations that went along with that kind of notoriety. I didn't need anything to puff me up at the time. There were too many other things to work on in me. God knew. I just trusted the Peace-Factor. I didn't have peace about taking on the contract for the Coke jingle, no matter what God's reason was for saying "No." He wasn't keeping me from blessings and cool opportunities. He was keeping me from the rest of it – whatever "it" was. **Peace protects**. We can trust God's peace.

God in Math

Before finishing my first full year, I knew God was calling me to return the following year. I was now very much aware of why God had called me to the school. His blessings for my obedience were exponential. I had recorded on many albums and traveled through Ecuador, Peru, Columbia, and even Guatemala. I returned a third year just in time for the teacher's conference. It was my first one. I didn't know exactly what to expect but I was glad to be a part. We had the most outstanding executive director, Doctora Carola. She was excellence personified. I'm not sure if she was even five feet tall but she carried herself as if she were a general, very stately and tremendously dignified. She made you want to make her proud. You couldn't help but long for personal excellence after spending time in her presence. She had the greatest sense of humor and a most gregarious laugh to match. My kind of gal! I had the utmost of respect for her. Carola held the highest standards not because of her faith in humans but because of her great faith in God. He took preeminence in everything, right down to every academic subject.

The teacher's conference was no exception. We were there to show God in all things. As a matter of fact, one day during the conference she asked that we split into groups of five or less. There were at least 20 of us. She appointed us a subject and asked that we discuss how God could be demonstrated in that subject. Then she asked us to choose a leader who would express the details we had concluded. My group's subject was math. We went around in circles trying to come up with where we could find math in the Bible. Noah's Ark, the two- by- two's, and the Tower of Babel came up. Afterward, Carola asked us to choose a leader. Everyone pointed to me. I was surprised because Spanish was my second language. I figured they would have wanted someone a little more eloquent. I prayed, "Lord, help me not make my group look stupid and anoint me; if you can, anoint me to speak about math." I heard the Lord specifically say, "Go to the beginning." I pulled out my bilingual Bible and shuffled to Genesis chapter 1. I then heard Carola say, "Okay, Matematicas." (Math) I felt this wave of panic as I stood up. I had not quite gotten what God was trying to show me; but, I decided to just go ahead and share the basic details of our conversation and then read the scripture. "Let's just go to the beginning" I echoed. I could see my group wondering where I was going with all this since we hadn't discussed it. I decided not to look in their direction for a moment as I took my leap of faith into Genesis.

I read verse one, "In the beginning God created the heavens and the earth." I stopped and said, "Hmm, there was nothing and then God added the heavens and the earth, Addition."

I continued, "Verse two. And the earth was without form, and void; and darkness was upon the face of the deep. And the Spirit of God moved upon the face of the waters." I pointed out enthusiastically, "God moved! There was velocity... speed... and... numbers!" Wow! That made sense. Cool! I thought that was pretty good, so I kept going.

"Verse three. And God said, Let there be light: and there was light." I interjected, "He added again." I kept reading, "And God saw the light, that it was good: and God divided the light from the darkness." I caught on... "Division!" I started to see things a little differently. God was creating space, adding, dividing, and now we had a first, the first day. Firsts...

I started to get excited. I'll never forget reading the next few verses. As revelation came, I turned around to the dry eraser board and began to draw some lines. I hadn't planned to write a thing, but here it came... "North! South! East! West! 0, 1,2,3,4, -1, -2, -3, -4. Longitude! Latitude! Lines! Spheres! Geometry! Circles! Squares! Triangles! Addition! Multiplication! Subtraction!" There was a detailed graph before me. I felt like I was going to explode! It was the most anointed math moment I ever knew! When I turned around to look at them all, Carola jumped to her feet and exclaimed, "THIS IS GOD IN MATH!"

It was hysterical because I was standing there feeling like a total idiot one minute and an utter genius the next. It was true! It was God... God in Math! Dios en las Matematicas!

Pearl Power

It's amazing what the prayer "Help," accompanied by a leap of faith, can produce. You just never know until you try it! God sure is super smart!

Chief and Commander

While traveling to Bolivia with a group of Ecuadorian pastors and our worship band, I found myself once again in the Quito International Airport. I was the only female. Not a typical cultural situation for Latin America; but, I wasn't a typical missionary and they all knew it. I could hold my own.

As we checked in, the attendant asked if I would mind being moved to first class, explaining that economy was a little too full. I gladly accepted under the one condition that I could have a couple of my pastor friends join me. She agreed, and by the time we all asked for the same favor, we had about six of our team members in first class. Nothing like favor!

This was an unusual trip because while we were leaving Ecuador there was news of a Border War stirring up between Ecuador and Peru. Peru was our next stop. We had a layover in Lima and watched in dismay as the army planes were getting ready to respond to the situation. That was only half of the concern as there was also evidence of some upheaval and even a revolution in Bolivia, our final destination.

We planned to be careful and steer clear of those challenged areas, sticking to our mission. Upon arrival we were handed coca tea for altitude sickness. That's the same plant used to make cocaine. I thought that was interesting. It was suppose to help you acclimate. I just felt a little lightheaded. Not sure the tea helped, but it was a nice gesture. La Paz sits at 13,000 feet above sea level and you feel it, even coming from the Andes mountain range of 10,000 feet in Quito.

That very first day, even before we had the opportunity to minister or get settled into our accommodations, my parents were calling to make sure everything was okay. They had seen the news about Ecuador, Peru and Bolivia and were concerned. When my mother called the house where I was staying, a distinguished voice answered in perfect English. My mom was a little surprised and took advantage of the moment to ask how I was doing and if I was safe. The woman replied, "This is the home of the Chief and Commander of the Armed Forces of Bolivia. Your daughter is in the best of care." I was JUST fine!

As we traveled through Bolivia, we experienced the rich culture, breathtaking views, and welcoming hearts. We had poured ourselves out in ministry and saw many people come to know Jesus and the freedom that comes from believing his Word. It was awesome.

One day as we pulled our long coach bus up to the next town I could sense something was different. My spirit felt disturbed and I decided to start fasting. As I dropped my things off at the home where I would be staying, I felt uneasy. We were spread out this time. I was staying at a home with a couple of other band members. When I stuck my head out of my room I saw the church's young, single worship leader flirting, in a disturbing way, in a hallway with the married hostess. I dodged back in my room and I began to pray. That evening when we gathered for the service I could feel an uneasiness. Things were not right. **You can't pretend everything is hunky dory when it's just not. Deception comes when a truth is traded for a lie. It leaves room for all kinds of havoc.** Later that evening I learned that the town was known for witchcraft. No wonder. The enemy had gotten a foothold, even in the church.

It was eleven o'clock at night by the time the service had ended and they were serving dinner. Goat's brain was on the menu. I was glad to be fasting. By the time they dropped us off it was midnight, but no one was at my guest home. We rang the doorbell multiple times. No answer.

They decided to drop everyone else off and try again. Now it was 1:00am. Still no response. The driver got desperate. He didn't know what to do so he dropped us off at a motel in the red-light district. It cost $1 a room, if that. It was a two-story building. All the room doors were directly to the outside. Mine was on the second story on the end. There were a few prostitutes waiting on one side and a guy selling cocaine on the other. I couldn't believe we were actually doing this. As I walked through, I could feel the weight of the place. I made my way up the stairs with the two other guys behind me. They watched me to my room. As I passed the public bathroom I noticed urine, feces, and toilet paper scattered all over the floor. It was horrendous.

I walked into the room, locked the door, and immediately took a small table and pushed it under the door handle. I added a chair and anything else I could get my hands on. The room was aqua blue – not a great color for peace. I noticed a potato sack blanket on the bed. It was a very cold night. There was no heat. I flipped it over checking for bugs and then laid down, pulling it ever so carefully over my coat and shoes. I had left the light on intentionally. I looked around the room in disbelief and heard some gunshots down below. As I closed my eyes I felt a huge tear fall over my nose and onto the hard pillow. Immediately I heard the Lord say, "No." It was firm, but it was kind. I didn't hear God audibly, but right down in my spirit. He said, "I am the same with you here as I was at the house of the Chief and Commander of the Armed Forces. Nothing has changed. You are safe." I then fell asleep.

The next day the pastors came for me at 6:00am. They were mortified, apologizing profusely, but I was really okay. I actually slept hard. They brought me to the home where I was supposed to be staying. I told the husband and wife that I was concerned about them and that God wanted to heal their marriage. They sat on the side of my bed crying. I asked them to hold hands and pray. They did! We stayed one more night and I believe God turned some things around. I kept fasting until we were back on the bus and exiting the town. I didn't want to take anything extra with me

Pearl Power

Discerning someone else's struggle or weakness is a call to prayer. God can help any situation. Praying for someone is our best strategy to help because we are asking God to intervene. Prayer is our partnership with God to get his work done on the earth. He needs us to pray. The Bible says our prayers are powerful and effective, like rockets to heaven. God hears our cry and responds right away. If someone asks for prayer, it is always better to pray for them on the spot rather than thinking you'll remember later. Later is not guaranteed. Besides, Scripture also tells us that when two people pray in agreement there is great power. Prayer is another superpower just like discernment. It's just a conversation with God. Don't get distracted by all the words. He's listening to your heart!

An Invitation to the Ball

One of my best friends from Ecuador, Gabriela, was from a very affluent family. Her father had run for the presidency just before I arrived in Quito. I always enjoyed her company because she was hungry for the things of God besides being fun-loving, humorous, and amazingly brilliant. Gabriela grew up going to church but now she had a desire to know God in a deeper way, to follow him, and to believe his Word. She seemed amazed by how I would talk about God as a natural part of everyday living. God was a part of everything I did. A lot of my conversation revolved around the last thing that happened because of God. There was no separation of God and the rest of my life being that my relationship with him was a continual conversation and a part

162

of how I saw everything working. Omniscient, omnipotent, omnipresent... he knows it all, he can do anything and everything, and he's always with me. That's my God!

Her father had just erected the latest five-star hotel and was about to have their inaugural ball. They invited me to sing at the event. I was told there would be a couple thousand guests in the ballroom where I would be singing. I just happened to have my bridesmaid gown from my brother Kieran's wedding. It was a deep emerald green, sleeveless dress. I was grateful I had something appropriate for the evening. So, like a good worship leader, I invited the church pianist who brought his keyboard. All I knew was worship songs. When we got there I was told there was a change of plans and that I would now be singing for a private mass with the country's top officials, diplomats and their wives. Sure, why not? It was all the same to me. Sing downstairs in the ballroom for Jesus, sing upstairs in the penthouse for Jesus.

The highest spiritual leader from their church, the Cardinal, came to do the mass. It was beautiful. He had all his special robes and accessories on with an extraordinarily high hat; but, behind all these garments you could feel a very genuine and sincere love for God. I loved that!

With the tall hat, he nodded carefully to me to come and sing. I moved forward slowly and sang *How Great Thou Art* in Spanish. He seemed pleased. I smiled and sat down. A few moments later he nodded again. I got back up, moved forward slowly, and sang *I Love You Lord* again in Spanish. I smiled and returned to my seat. Some time passed as he shared and followed the typical stages of the mass and then once again he nodded to me. Now I was getting amused. I had favor with the Cardinal. The good thing was that I wasn't going to run out of songs. I could keep telling my piano friend from church what was next and go with the flow. By the time it was all said and done I must have sung at least five songs. This was fun!

My prayer was that it would be anointed and that the Holy Spirit would move through the songs and touch people's hearts. I prayed that the people would feel God's presence and I believed that's just what God was doing. There was a peace that had settled in the room. In the midst of these top 80 officials and diplomats you could sense an awe and reverence for God. I felt very comfortable and sang with all my heart, hands lifted when I wanted to and lots of eye contact. Nothing to hide...

After the mass I shook hands with the Cardinal and thanked my pianist. As we made our way through the crowd, people were stopping me to thank me for the special music. One lady leaned over and privately said, "Cuando usted canto mi esposo comenzo a temblar. Que paso?" (When you began to sing my husband started to shake. What was that?) I told her that it was the presence of God. I was just amazed as she was. She smiled and didn't quite know what to do with the information so she thanked me and moved along. A few seconds later, another woman grabbed my arm; leaning into my ear, she said the same thing. Cuando usted canto mi esposo comenzo a temblar. When you began to sing my husband started to shake. She looked at me like, what is all this suppose to mean? I told her the same thing, "It was God's presence. He was responding to God's presence." I thought to myself, "There's nothing like a good healthy dose of the fear of God for people in influential positions." God had made himself known. Why they were shaking I did not know; but, I had read about it in the Bible and I had seen it before, just not at an inaugural ball among the affluent. Pretty cool!

By the end of the evening I counted six women who stopped me to tell me the same story. I was amazed. My mission was simply to worship the Lord with all my heart. There was not a drop of *the fear of man* present. I felt honored to be there and was respectful of those present, but it was all eyes on Jesus for me. I had absolutely nothing to lose. And then God came... and shook things up a little bit! Ha!

Pearl Power

We can't see what God is doing behind all the faces in our lives but we can trust that he is always at work. II Peter 3:9 says that God is patient and doesn't want anyone to perish but that all would come to repentance. This tells me that God is always looking for moments to draw people to himself. Scripture also says that He inhabits the praises of his people, meaning that when we worship him he comes in his manifest presence. Sometimes you can literally feel his presence. So, if you are in your car, the bus, on the street, in a store, anywhere...and you are worshipping God he will show up and not only touch your life but all those around you. That's some serious power!

TEN

Clicking My Heels and Heading Home

"Hope deferred makes the heart sick."
—Proverbs 13:12

In my last six months of living in Ecuador I began feeling homesick. It was more than usual. I was nearing twenty-five now and more aware of my biological clock. Twenty-five seemed monumental. I often climbed to the roof of the apartment building to talk to Jesus. "Where is he?" I would probe. "My man?!" Gazing over the city the tears would come streaming down my cheeks and I would ask the Lord to either take away the desire to be married or bring him quickly. These seemed like the only two options at the time. Then I would try to work out a deal. "Let me just meet him, Lord? Give me a clue. Anything. Okay, a sign. Am I getting married? Soon?" All I got was, "Trust me." This would have to be enough for me.

That spring a family friend came for a visit from Savannah, Georgia. Greg Carney was on a medical mission's trip. We had been friends for a few years now. He was a doctor just like my dad, Irish American, tall, handsome, and full of Southern gentility. He visited the previous year showing signs of interest but always remained respectful of my call to ministry and the work there in Quito. This time he brought his mother. Mrs. Carney was an absolute delight. While her son was in the jungle treating the sick and educating them on how to better care for themselves, the two of us took off for the mountains. I gave her my usual tour to the classic Indian town of Otavalo and we stayed at the most beautiful bungalow by a lake.

Mrs. Carney was not your typical Southern belle. Yes, she carried all the charm and demeanor of a diplomat's wife but she was real, down to earth, and full of adventure. She wore an amazing amount of precious stones and always dressed to the nines; yet, you never quite knew what would come next. She was inquisitive, fully engaged with the culture, and ready to try whatever opportunity provided. Not an ounce of trepidation. My kind of gal! Mrs. Carney was a true breath of fresh air to my tired and wearied soul. I liked this lady! And oh how being with her made me miss my mom!

When Greg returned from the jungle, many of the missionaries encouraged me to consider him as more than just a good friend. It was verifiable; we had a lot in common. He was a good man, loved the Lord, respected me, and was close to my family. My father loved him. What more could you ask for? I wondered if he was the one. One person actually called me "necia," (stubborn). I knew I was holding my ground, but I never thought I was being stubborn. Maybe I was? Maybe I should give it a shot? Perhaps this was one of those Isaac and Rebekah stories from the Old Testament where the servant goes to find the wife. Down deep I didn't feel more than a strong friendship. I really liked him but thought maybe love was something that grows rather than the "love at first sight" scenario. Well, whatever the case I figured I'd better do *something*! Twenty-five had just closed in on me. So, I told Greg we should try it out. His jaw dropped. Really? He was surprised knowing how defined I had been; but, we agreed to take a step into the possibility.

I waved good-bye and knew it would be a few months before I would see them again. What great people! They had great hearts, great love for God, and were extremely generous. They lavished me with love and made me feel like royalty. I appreciated each kind gesture and every bit of understanding. They sensed how very dear the ministry was to me and valued me as a person doing God's will. I had enjoyed every moment and treasured the time with Mrs. Carney. I thought, "Huh! I'd marry Greg just for the mother-in-law!" They both were stellar! But for now it would be long calls and lots of dreaming about the possibility of what this relationship held.

For months I planned my departure. I was truly home sick now, heart sick for home. My tears could be triggered on the slightest whim. I longed to be close to my family, to be in proximity, to share birthday parties and special holidays. There was a weight of separation. It had been seven months since I had seen them and almost three years of living overseas.

My work was complete. I had grown tremendously. In my giving I was filled. I knew I had fulfilled my mission. I was sad to leave but knew it was time. There were many going-away parties, dinners, and teas. All the churches loved on me, gave me gifts, and prayed over my life. We shared tears and laughter as we reflected on all the memories created. It had been a very busy few years. I had left my mark! People were changed. God had used my life. Now, once again, I was being sent off with a blessing. It was extremely humbling.

I had given away most of my clothes but still had a hard time zipping my suitcase from all the presents: wood carvings, leather bags, paintings, home decorations, alpaca blankets, tapestries, love notes with scriptures, blessings and prayers. It was overwhelming. Ecuador would always be in my heart.

But there was more. I longed for more and had great expectations about what came next. I had to find out what that meant, to chase God once again, to be still and know.

Pearl Power

You've heard it said, "Wise men still seek him". Yes, the wise men were looking for Jesus and they found him. The wisest thing we can do in this life is to seek God, to look for him in new and fresh ways. Challenges, changes and the unknown stir our hearts once again to get a road map of where we are headed. We can't see like God can but we can get glimpses as we seek him for his will. He said, "Call to me and I will answer you and tell you great and unsearchable things you do not know" —Jeremiah 33: 3.

Longing, Not Living

Being still came harder this time. Have you ever heard the saying? "Don't let your longing for the what is to come take away from your living today." Elizabeth Elliot, a famous Christian author and missionary to Ecuador would say that quite often. She wrote a book called Passion and Purity. I hung on her every word. She had abandoned herself to God at a young age. She longed for marriage but she committed herself to living in the present. When the time came she married. She said it was so very wonderful, more than what she could have imagined. I was amazed by her resolve. Even when Mr. Right did come, her heart still took refuge in the

"Shadow of the Almighty"- the title of the first book she wrote as her husband was murdered leaving her alone in a foreign land, Ecuador, with a little one. She picked herself back up and followed with total abandon once again, ministering to the very people who killed her beloved Jim Elliot. She never quit; she followed the call of God on her life with or without a spouse. Elizabeth was yielded and consecrated for the purpose of one thing, following Christ. I was amazed by her strength and fortitude in the midst of such trial and tragedy.

I struggled to live presently. I kept finding myself daydreaming about my wedding day, my dress, my ring, my future. My future would have to encompass many things: a husband, children, a ministry, and the nations. I longed for it all.

Before becoming a missionary I was working to complete all the pre-med courses needed for nursing. I knew that would be helpful on the mission field but I really didn't want to take blood from patients. So I considered chiropractic as I was thinking of all the ways I could meet the needs of the people. I was one course shy of completing all my pre-med requirements for chiropractic college but just didn't have a peace about it. My passion was in leading worship, ministering in churches and sharing my walk with God. I loved to inspire people.

Now here I was with a two-year Bible degree and three associate degrees from all my random studies: Math/Science, Sociology, and Humanities. I was still trying to figure out how this would all work. I decided the best thing to do was to finish my studies as a missionary and pull together what seemed like hundreds of credits for the Bachelor of Science in Missiology. Yes, there is such a degree; and, no it has nothing to do with missiles. Ha!

I arrived back in New York just in time to register at Nyack College. The missions director was extremely gracious and they accepted all my credits. I would finish in just one year and then move on with my life, do the next big thing... hopefully get married.

Just a month after arriving in the States my mother and I decided to take a trip to visit the Carneys in Georgia. I had spent many hours on the phone with Greg over the previous four months. In my transparency, I'm sure he felt my longing to settle down. He was hoping for the same. This trip was filled with hopes, dreams, and more longing for the future. He had a house on an island off the coast of Savannah. The drive alone was breathtaking. Spanish moss swayed in the breeze off every great ancient tree. As usual, his family was extremely gracious and I was swept off my feet. The city was filled with romance, from sweet Southern accents, to the historical sites and architecture. It was dreamy. The crab legs, corn on the cob doused in liquid butter, and boiled potatoes abounded. There seemed to be much potential and great promise. The conversation changed to solidifying hopes and settling the "wishful thinking." Greg, always a gentleman, let me know I would be free to minister and to even go on missions trips. He wanted me to be happy. He wanted this to work.

After settling into college for the last round of studies, my age seemed to be all the more magnified. Going back to school at 25, after living on the mission field and ministering in 17 different nations, was weird. I was neither here, nor there. I didn't quite fit. I certainly hadn't arrived but I was moving forward. I had seen so much. No one really knew who I was, where I had come from, or what I was about. Once again I had to work my way in, to build trust, to just "be" until the Lord opened opportunity for me to minister. Thank God it was only a hop, skip, and jump across the

Hudson River to my folks' house. I would go home on the weekends and minister at churches every chance I was offered. By this time, I was slightly more recognized in the Spanish Christian music world because of all the recordings I had been a part of. I had begun to receive more ministry engagements. I was still being asked to sing in Central and South America; yet, I could only take those trips that worked with my study schedule – in other words, very few.

About a month into school, Greg called and asked if I could take a long weekend. That sounded like a great idea! He had planned a trip with his family to visit his brother in the San Juan Islands off the coast of Seattle, Washington. Once we had arrived in Seattle the family chartered a plane to take us out to the islands. I was severely impressed! What a gorgeous place on the face of the earth. Greg's sister-in-law had made fresh blueberry pie from the berries picked in the backyard. Woohoo! The rocky beaches and general topography were magnificent. It was a thrill to experience the raw natural beauty of this place. On the second day we overlooked the ocean from these stunning cliffs. Greg climbed down the rugged terrain and made his way out to the rocky beach. He called for me to join him. As I reached his spot he turned and said, "I found a rock!" All of a sudden I realized what was happening. Oh my! He had a family heirloom in his hand. A rock indeed! The rest became a blur as I stared at my hand. Once again I started dreaming of going down the aisle. It was finally happening. I was twenty-five, a quarter of a century, and I would be a bride. It was time to buy those magazines, to look at dresses, and to plan my future.

I was happy. I felt like I was getting somewhere; but, I remember trying to find a place to get alone with God, to journal, and to dream – still not quite present. It was all about what came next and not about where I actually was, who I was with, and how this was part of the kingdom plan. I just wanted it done already, to get on with my life!

When I returned home I started planning the engagement party. I wanted everyone to know and be a part. The following month, the Carneys flew up and we had a big *to do* – crystal and silver, and everything else you can imagine. I was feeling like things were coming together. It was happening, right? Yet, somewhere along the way I started to realize that I didn't have as much peace as I had hoped. I hadn't really been paying much attention. I was so wrapped up in what I was hoping would take place that I had skipped over some of the gentle nudges in my spirit. My feelings of moving to the next step of life had been running ahead and now I questioned how this was truly supposed to look.

I reasoned that we were both kind-hearted people, steady and faithful. We would have a good marriage and never divorce, no matter what. Besides, I was 25 and this might be my last opportunity. I felt old, especially around the college kids; but, something was amiss. I figured I would catch up to it, whatever *it* was.

By November, I began looking for counsel. Maybe someone else had been in my shoes and could talk me down this road to the altar. I didn't want to disappoint my dad. He seemed quite content with the whole arrangement. That's it! Maybe it was more of like an arranged marriage, back to Isaac and Rebekah.

To my absolute amazement, Elizabeth Elliot was scheduled to speak at our college women's conference. The Elizabeth Elliot, my hero! And guess who was asked to lead worship? That's right! Yours truly! Excellent, I would ask Elizabeth Elliot for counsel. Surely she would understand my plight. We had so much in common. I would find a moment after the conference and seek her out. Yay God! You know just who to bring. Of all the people on the face of the earth,

Elizabeth Elliott would be my first pick. I trusted her words, her testimony, and her character. She was strong, but real. I knew we would connect and see this thing eye-to-eye.

Sure enough, Elizabeth came; she shared a powerful message and we were all very moved. Wouldn't you know, just as I had secretly planned, she was sitting signing books and I saw what looked like an advantageous moment. This was it! I would speak to her about my upcoming nuptial engagement, arrangement, whatever... She would understand me.

I noticed she was quite focused on the task at hand, but I felt like it was now or never. "Elizabeth," I piped up sliding in beside her. "My name is Fiona Delamere and I too was a missionary to Ecuador." For some reason she didn't seem impressed; yet, I forged on, explaining my current situation and trying to get her up to date on my life. She didn't budge. Finally, after realizing she didn't want to be friends and wasn't looking for any particular emotional connection, I clearly stated my quandary, remarking that perhaps I was like a Rebekah and Greg was my Isaac. She looked down at my ring, then raised her head and met me eye-to-eye. With undeniable conviction and severity, she delivered a message that hit me to my core. "I can't believe you would even consider marrying this man. He does not have the same call of God on his life!" With that she turned her back to me.

Oh no! Oh Jesus, Help! My head dropped. Hot tears streamed down my face as I raced out of the conference center. I was humiliated and obviously shaken. Oh God, oh God! What to do? What do I do, Lord? Run to the chaplain's office. He is a kind man. He will understand.

It was true. Pastor Pletnicks was a gentle soul yet absolutely Spirit-led, as well as extremely gracious. He wouldn't waste words. At least his words would be diplomatic. I trusted he would steer me in the right direction.

"Elizabeth Elliott is a mean woman" I bellowed.

"What happened?!"

I returned with equal surprise – tears and drama. "She said she couldn't believe I would even consider marrying Greg and that he doesn't have the same call of God on his life!"

"Wow, that *is* pretty direct."

"I was so embarrassed. I wasn't expecting all *that*!"

"Well, next week is Missions Week. Why don't we commit to praying about it. Let's just give it the week and see what is on God's heart. Surely God has a plan."

My life verse, Jeremiah 29:11, popped up in my spirit, "For I know the plans I have for you, declares the Lord, plans to prosper you and not to harm you, plans to give you hope and a future." The future was what I seemed most concerned about; but, I had to sit myself down and be honest about what God was trying to say to me presently. It didn't take a week for me to conclude that I had truly lost my peace and that what Elizabeth said only confirmed what was registering in my spirit. I was just so terribly disappointed. How would I talk to Greg about this? What would I tell Dad? All I ever wanted was to be approved by my dad, showing him I had clear direction in life and get his blessing. I thought, "What about all the people at the engagement party and all those gifts?" I would have to give everything back. Yikes! How humiliating! I couldn't quite get my head around it. Maybe I could settle. Maybe I wasn't hearing clearly. Surely there was an easier way. I really wasn't up for rocking the boat. Besides, by this time Greg had bought me a white Jeep with gold pinstripes and then there was the house that was waiting on the island. This was no small feat! How could I disappoint all the people hanging on this event – all the people who were believing and hoping.

The very next weekend Greg came up to the Northeast for a neurology conference. We met in Pennsylvania where I was able to stay with friends. That Sunday I suggested we attend the church they pastored. The Garretts were old friends of my family. They led worship at the summer conferences we attended. I always wanted to have a family like theirs. Five kids all playing an instrument, singing and worshipping the Lord. For years, that had been my dream. I wanted a big ministry family. They were my prime example.

Maybe they would have some insight. Perhaps I could speak with Mom Garrett as Greg chatted with Dad Garrett and we could come to some similar understanding. They invited us back to their home for lunch, a big Sunday supper as usual, with the whole family gathered. My plan was working. As we entered their home, I saw Mrs. Garrett grab a box of crackers, some cheese and apples and said, "You two follow me. I'm taking you to the prophet's chamber." Hmm? We proceeded up the stairs to a brand new apartment they had just added onto their home for visiting ministers. It was lovely. She then added, "I think you two have some things to talk about. Take your time. This will be good for you." Oh Lordy... Yes, we did have some things to share. I was hoping I could just pretend everything was dandy; but, I had this gut-wrenching clarity about what was about to ensue.

Greg wasn't expecting this conversation. This made it all the more difficult to address the unrest in my heart. How did I get this far without true peace? How did I get both of us here? I sure had pushed my own will. **Living in the future was blinding.** All I could see was the ring, the dress, and walking the aisle. He sincerely acknowledged my dilemma and asked if we could take a couple of weeks to prayerfully consider what to do. I agreed. It was the least I could offer.

That week I was restless. I had two vivid dreams. One was about my visit to the shop where I had picked out my actual wedding dress. I entered on a friendly note and smiled as I explained that I could not purchase the dress at present but would be back someday. The second dream was a bit more dramatic, as the ring had fallen off my finger and the diamond had cracked in half. The diamond was black on the inside.

That was it. I knew I could not go through with it. I decided to visit my dad the very next day during office hours. This could not wait another minute. Upon my arrival he offered me an adjustment, which seemed like just the right thing. He could see I was stressed out. As I lay down on the chiropractic table I wanted to ease my way into the conversation; but, the words failed me and tears escaped down my cheeks. I tried to get a few words out and all of a sudden he caught on. What is this about? Then, connecting the dots, I heard, "Oh Fiona, You don't have to marry Greg." I bawled my eyes out. It was not pretty. Finally pulling myself together I explained how I didn't want to be a disappointment. He assured me that peace was the right thing to follow and we would have to trust God.

When the two weeks came to a close, Greg and I talked it through. It was not what he hoped for but he was truly understanding and amazingly respectful. It was actually hard to take. It would have been so much easier if he had just been a real jerk and I had some serious offense or at least *something* negative to say. Ah see! That's why! But no, the only thing missing was peace and that had to be enough.

Shortly after we hung up the phone, Greg's mom called. Oh what an absolutely outstanding human being. She blessed me, literally, affirming my call to ministry and assured me she was not angry, but understood where I was coming from. Oh what precious saints! Unbelievable! Was that as smooth as I think it was? The grace to do what was right came in buckets, and then waves that overtook me. The weight of the world came off my shoulders. I did the right thing. Married or not married, God had a plan. I was sticking to it.

Pearl Power

It's always nice when we get things right and reap the benefits of good choices. But, oh the absolute joy it is after having made serious mistakes, and falling flat on our faces to turn in humility and accept the truth. It seems like this particular joy is greater because it comes with such restoration from God and redeems a broken moment. The joy of humbling ourselves before God so far exceeds the shame that would want to hold us captive to our failures. God rejoices so greatly over our restoration and submission to truth. Like the prodigal son, he'll throw a party every time for our return to truth.

An Unexpected Ministry

So, here I was, once again, unattached and free to take any and every opportunity afforded. I would pour into the people around me and finish up the year with dignity, by the grace of God. Surely we would keep this to ourselves.

What always amazes me is that God can use just about anything. Wouldn't you know, it wasn't long before word got around campus that I was now *unengaged*. What a title. The emphasis was not placed on my status or availability as much as what I had accomplished. You would think I would be considered demoted; but no, students were watching.

There were engaged couples questioning whether or not they should go through with it. Really God? Can't we just keep this thing on the hush hush? Nope, not a chance. Not just one, but three couples sought me out within the next few months to talk about why I did what I did. They weren't sure they were doing the right thing either. Yes, I actually had a ministry to help the peace-less engaged couples get unengaged. Go figure! What a ministry...

Pearl Power

Once again, God uses things that are broken. If it's a part of your life, it's a part of your testimony and at some point God can use it for his glory if you are willing to hand it over. The truth is, I actually helped people by telling them how I messed up and then how I got back on track. Don't discount the broken moments of your story. Sometimes sharing them is part of the process of coming full circle and receiving your full healing.

Embracing the Present

After the dust settled and I fully embraced my present, I realized how much I truly enjoyed ministry. It was a passion. I was now getting asked more frequently to sing and share the main message at all different types of churches, Spanish and English speaking alike, traditional and charismatic. It didn't matter to me as long as it was Bible-based and there was freedom to share. I would seek the Lord for a word for that particular congregation, recall testimonies that applied to that word, and ask God for some specifics to minister effectively. I also fasted and spent hours praying and seeking God for what was on his heart. That year I was amazed at God's favor and grace. New doors were opening in the city and I felt honored to be trusted in this way.

On one particular trip into Queens I was asked to sing some solos and preach. After the service I did a typical altar call asking for recommitment and a call to seeking God once again. The altar was flooded. I figured I would invite the pastor and elders to join me in praying, but they nodded for me to just go ahead and pray. I started on one side of the church and realized God was giving me special words for the people, specific details, and a certainty that it was divinely inspired. I spoke with authority as hands went up. Some knelt, some stood, some began to weep. I thought maybe God was done, but every time I laid my hands on someone the words would come and I would bravely state what bubbled up in my spirit. By this time it had been an hour and a half or so and I had only reached the first two rows of people, a good hundred. Others were standing behind waiting for their own special word. The pastor leaned over and said that the next service would be coming in from the church that rented the building in the afternoon but that we could move to another room. I agreed. Sure, why not? I didn't have any other plans, plus hearing God was just fine with me. People's lives were being touched, Jesus was revealed. It was amazing! I enjoyed the whole process. I knew it was God. I was simply the vessel, a willing vessel; and, the people were patient.

We reconvened in a classroom and God gave me the strength and impartation for 50 more. Only God could know what was precious and important to all these hearts. Only he could give a word that would change it all, reignite their faith and let them know he truly cared. He was personal. For some, it was about their marriage; for others, it was their children or the ones they longed for. All of it was hopeful and edifying. I noticed some take great comfort in the words, while others sat quietly just receiving. We were in awe at what appeared to be a moment of revival. God was reawakening hearts. We all felt humbled by the experience. It was astounding.

One thing I had learned early on in ministry was basically, *not* to take it all in. There was no room for taking credit. I would hold it out at a distance knowing God's glory was not to be hampered with. Scripture was clear about these precepts. Man could not handle claiming the glory of God. Taking glory could actual destroy a ministry. This was nothing to fool with. Each ministry moment was another bouquet of flowers to be handed right back to God. I could never take credit for what he was doing in the life of another. I couldn't take it personally. It was obvious God was working in a supernatural way. My joy and reward was the sheer pleasure of being the vessel he used. This was sacred.

Pearl Power

God wants to do powerful things in and through our lives. He loves to use people who are not concerned about who will get the credit. When amazing things happen we should tell people it was all God... after all, it is!

Snickers

One very fresh memory takes me back to a trip I made into Brooklyn. It was an awesome day. God showed up in hundreds of ways. I was now tired and just wanted a Snickers and a nap. Oh the simplicity of being twenty something, single, unattached and fully able to take naps when I felt like it. It was a long drive home, the sky was gray, and the rain came and went in drizzles. This only confirmed my need to snuggle up in a blanket and drift off. Ministry always pulled every little bit out of me. You figure, you are exerting yourself physically, emotionally, and spiritually; and, when the power of God would come down it would leave you like a wet noodle by the end of the day. No wonder the pastor's day off is Monday. There's a reason for that. He's whipped!

As I approached my town I thought of where I could buy a Snickers. Any proper gas station in the U.S. would surely stock Snickers. I made my approach taking a route that would achieve the projected goal – fill up the tank and purchase my precious Snickers.

As I climbed the main thoroughfare I noticed an older gentleman half way up the hill. He had some grocery bags in one hand and his thumb up with the other. The mist was closing in again. As I passed him I had a funny feeling that my ministry moments had not been completed for the day. I was almost home! I had been driving for two hours. The blanket was calling. I decided that if he was still there after my stop at the gas station that I would pick him up. I was pretty sure he wouldn't be. Stopping, I hooked up the gas tank and ran into the station eager to make my investment in a longing fulfilled... a Snickers.

"No Snickers!" the man confirmed.

"No Snickers? Are you sure? How is that possible?"

What kind of business are we running here? I speculated.

But it was true. There wasn't a Snickers anywhere to be found. Trust me, I searched.

So, down the hill I went again, only to find Mr. Grocery Bags, thumb still up but now slightly on the soggy side. The rain was falling steadily. I pulled the car around to his side of the busy street and motioned for him to hop in. He was the most grateful soul I had met in a long time. As he made his way into the seat and turned to give me a semi-toothless grin, I noticed what looked like Campbell's Minestrone Soup in the corners of his mouth. It was orange and oily. I decided not to focus on that particular aspect of his face. Smiling, I asked where he was headed and he quickly mentioned my connecting street. Wow, that worked out just fine. We were a good five miles away. I was glad to pick him up. It would have taken him light years to walk the distance.

As I drove, he shared his life story. He was a Vietnam Vet. He had been through a lot. I reminded him of his daughter. I caught a tear in his eye at one point but thought it would be best to make him laugh instead. He seemed like he had carried enough for one lifetime. We were well past my folks' house when I realized he lived a few more miles away. It was a very long road. My mother always said if someone asks you to go a mile, go with them twain. She added that if you were going to bless a person, they should really feel blessed.

So I was committed to the journey. We sang a few patriotic tunes and then he pointed to a side street. "You can just drop me off here," he said. I assured him this was a door-to-door service and that I could take him the whole way. He hesitated and then agreed. As we dodged potholes along the muddy driveway and pulled up to the big house, I realized it was a half-way home. I made sure to keep smiling even though my heart had sunk. He had a hard life. I told him that God loved him and that he was keeping watch over him. As he opened his door he turned back, leaned over and landed a big wet kiss on my cheek. I tried not to think about the soup on the corners of his mouth. Then, reaching into his grocery bag, he pulled out a king-size Snickers bar. Oh for heaven's sake! God made it clear that day, if I would just take care of the people, he would take care of me. I was convinced.

Pearl Power

It's a real test when you are willing to bless those who could never pay you back. Helping other people get to their destination is always a part of getting to your own. You will move forward in leaps and bounds when you sacrifice to help others. It's an awesome principle. All of heaven comes out to cheer you on in your own personal life when you make other people a priority.

ELEVEN

Taking Captive Every Thought

"We demolish arguments and every pretension that
sets itself up against the knowledge of God and we take
captive every thought to make it obedient to Christ."
—II Corinthians 10:5

After a very full year, I finally graduated. I had been
spinning quite a few plates at one time. It was nice to be
done and to have a chunky diploma with my name on it. I
had completed the task. I had come full circle. I felt accomplished. It was now the summer of 1996.

What came next I really could not have been prepared
for. I was ready for some rest after all the final pushes of
college graduation; but, what transpired brought me to a
place I would not wish on my worst enemy. It came like a
whirlwind. I can only describe it as spiritual wickedness just
as it says in Ephesian 6:12. "For our struggle is not against
flesh and blood, but against the rulers, against the authori-
ties, against the powers of this dark world and against the
spiritual forces of evil in the heavenly realms."

I was not a stranger to spiritual attacks. I had witnessed
plenty of things that could only be explained in spiritual
terms; yet, one day, shortly after graduation, a battle began
to rage in my mind. Recalling it makes the hair on my arms

want to stand. It was as if every filthy demon out of hell was throwing the most ungodly, vile, and perverse thoughts at me. I was used to rebuking the enemy. I knew my authority in Christ and I knew if I just worshipped the Lord the enemy would have to flee. If need be, according to the word of God, I would bind those things that I could discern. I could make a quick turnaround in my thoughts when I had something come up on the radar that was evil; but, this battle raged day and night for 30 days. It didn't matter how many times I rebuked the enemy. The filth kept coming. My dear friend Jeannie came to visit and in an attempt to help, she asked if I could describe it. All I could do was weep and tell her that it was so gross and so ungodly that I couldn't repeat any of it. I didn't want another soul to experience the anguish. Disturbing didn't even cut it. It was like flipping the channel all day. I had to constantly change my thoughts and hone in on something clean.

During this trying time, was when I got a hold of the scripture verse in II Corinthians 10:3-5, "For though we live in the world, we do not wage war as the world does. The weapons we fight with are not the weapons of this world. On the contrary, they have divine power to demolish strongholds. We demolish arguments and every pretension that sets itself up against the knowledge of God, and we take captive every thought to make it obedient to Christ."

So often I had thought the battle was out before me; but, now I recognized the greatest battle was in my own mind. God was helping me grasp how to fight effectively. I would quote with confidence, "I take captive every thought and make it obedient to Christ." I fought hard, realizing these were not my thoughts and chose to move away from them. Instead I pictured Jesus interceding for me. I thought of the angels fighting on my behalf. "The angels of the Lord encamp around those who fear Him." I kept taking the thoughts captive, grabbing a hold of them and making them do what I wanted. I can't even call them my thoughts. They weren't. I kept rebuking the enemy, reading the word out loud, worshipping God, and asking the Lord to cleanse me over and over. One day it all broke like a heavy metal chain being split in two. It was over. The night had passed. I had overcome.

People have asked why I think that happened. The only thing I can think of is that God wanted to make me stronger, to search Scripture for verses that I could apply to my situation, and to be able to share my experience with others who struggle in their thought-life. It would have to be usable for God to allow it. Overcoming a mental challenge by getting to Jesus certainly brings him glory. That'll work for me. I never struggled like that again.

Pearl Power

"The Lord is a refuge for the oppressed, a stronghold in times of trouble. Those who know your name will trust in you, for you, Lord have never forsaken those who seek you."— Psalms 9:9-10

Clarity

I watched in the coming months how God was opening more strategic opportunities in the Spanish-speaking world. There was a Christian artist named Marco Barrientos who invited me to sing on a couple of his recordings in Mexico City. I was honored to have the privilege. I actually stayed at his parents' house for the month. While I was there I would take walks around the gated community and study the beautiful homes. Each one was unique. One day as I rounded a corner I noticed a pink-colored stucco home with large birdcages on the driveway, considerably close to the sidewalk. I felt the urge to stop and observe. As I watched the many birds flying around I noticed that the yellow ones returned to their yellow partners and the green ones returned to their green partner as did the blue ones. As I stood there I realized God was trying to give me some clarity. I had been wondering if I would marry someone outside of my culture, if we would have the same first language, if we would look similar or completely opposite. Since I had traveled so much, I had the joy of experiencing many other cultures; I was drawn to them. It left me wondering what my husband would look like, what my children would look like, and how much we would hold in common. I was willing to embrace whatever God offered. Trust me!

Then it came in a gentle yet obvious revelation. I heard in my spirit, "Your husband will be from the same culture, speak the same language, carry the same calling, and you will compliment each other in your giftings and talents. You will have more in common than not." Well, that was that. It was settled. God had a plan and it would unfold in his timing. There was a Gringo with my name on him! I was glad to have a heads up!

Pearl Power

Sometimes God gives us clues. He knows when we need another ounce of hope and inspiration. We hold these things loosely as only time will tell the truth of what we believe we have discerned. After all, we can't see the big picture until it all comes into focus. We see things in part, slightly blurry, as the Scripture tells us. But eventually, God would make the rest known.

Sorpresa! Surprise!

While I was still in Ecuador a few years earlier, Jim called on me one evening. He and Mary were having dinner with a visiting pastor named Richard Mojica. Richard was from Nicaragua but lived in Miami. Jim introduced us and said "Sing something Fiona." I was a bit surprised but gladly obliged.

"Anything?"

"Sure, anything."

I decided to sing the last thing I had written, a sweet but soulful worship song. I could see Richard's eyes get big. He was not only a pastor but a worship leader, professional musician, and the head of a worship group that ministered all over Latin America. Back in Nicaragua, Richard's dad was the king of salsa in the '60s. Richard inherited his dad's amazing musical abilities. He was just about to finish up his latest record and asked if I would consider going to record in Miami. I told him I was heading that way for Christmas and would be passing through to New York. We set it up; I met his wife and beautiful children and sang a few solos on the project – another miracle that started at Jim and Mary's. The truth was I was rare. I loved singing Black gospel in Spanish. What are the chances! That wasn't common, especially coming from a redheaded Irish American. God was having fun!

Subsequent to the beginning of the initial project, Richard invited me to join his group for other concerts. After leaving Ecuador, we kept in touch and I sang on a few other records. When I graduated from college I had a lot of flexibility with my schedule. I started globetrotting a bit. We did concerts in Canada, the US, El Salvador, Nicaragua, Guatemala, Peru, and Colombia.

Early one hot Sunday morning in Managua, Nicaragua (try saying that five times fast), I had a headache. I had been speaking Spanish for two weeks straight with no reprieve. The worship band I was ministering with was comprised of three Nicaraguan brothers. They were a lot of fun – good godly men. But I was just done! I told the Lord I wanted to spend the afternoon talking to him in English. After ministering at the church service I planned to give myself a break. I was quickly making my way to the side door when I heard the pastor call out to me, "Hermana Fiona." I turned to tell him about my plan when he said, "Tenemos una sorpresa para ti!" (We have a surprise for you!) "Ohhhh, help!" I thought. But they were precious and so excited. The whole point of the trip was to minister – so off I went. We took a ride to Lake Granada. It's the only place in the world that you can find fresh water sharks. Out we went in a sweet gondola-looking boat that had a pretty canopy over the top. It was lovely. The pastor and his wife just smiled at me. We weren't talking. I thought, "How nice!" It seemed like they knew I needed a break. The lake is huge with some 400 *isletas* or little islands around its periphery. Some of the islands are so small they can only hold a tiny aluminum box-shaped shanty. Others are very elaborate with landscape and beautifully built homes. It was quite the tour from one extreme to the next. I was glad to be quiet, enjoying the peace and tranquility of the water and the views. It was like an ocean. You couldn't see to the other side.

As we took a turn cutting between two islands, I noticed a pretty little white house with a dock stretched out in the water. There was an older gentleman at the end of the dock looking out in our direction. All of a sudden I heard him yell toward the house, "Oh look, honey! It's a redhead!" I sat up in disbelief and yelled out, "You speak English?" Then turning to the pastor and his wife who now had huge grins, I heard "Sorpresa!" Surprise indeed!

What a great surprise it was! God is just too good! He knew how desperate I was. We pulled up to the dock and I jumped out to shake hands and find out what was going on with these two gringos. They told how they didn't speak Spanish and they hadn't talked to anyone else in over five months. They were taking care of the island while the missionary couple who owned it was in the States on furlough. We talked really fast for about two hours, trying to get in every detail. It was hilarious! I felt absolutely spoiled and was reminded how God knows my needs and would provide!

Lista? Ready?

One thing I knew, God would always take care of me. I may not have known how, where, or when, but I knew I just needed to trust and be ready, "Lista!"

The heat in Managua was hard to take on this particular trip. There was no air conditioner or fan. I literally shuffled into the shower in the middle of the night with my pajamas on, drenched myself with cold water, and then laid down on my bed staring at the ceiling while beads of sweat ran down my head and back. It didn't help that I had thick hair down to my waist. It was all up, at the top of my head, in the most enormous bun. I was baking!

The next day we headed out to the town square where we would be ministering. As the band set up, we waited for the electricity to be turned on. I stood there watching hundreds of people gather in the heat and humidity. My Irish American skin needed a break from the sun. I had prayed that God would connect the dots (freckles) on my arms and legs because I loved how tan the people around me could get. As usual, I turned beet red. I called it the "langosta her-bida" effect. I looked like a boiled lobster.

There was no telling how long it would take to get the power up. I thought to myself, "Man, I could just use a nice cold shower right now." Any time was a good time for a shower in Managua!

Just then a precious little woman came up to me and said, "Ven a mi casa. Esta cerca. Tengo una ducha!" (Come to my home. It's close by. I have a shower!) It was an unusual conversation; but, considering what I had just thought, it sounded like an answer to prayer! I smiled and said, "Bueno!" Alrighty then! Now we're talking!

As we entered the front door off the main street, there was a dirt floor open-air space with no roof in the center of their home. The rooms all jutted off this main area in a U shape with a nice wide porch connecting it all. The woman was so proud to have me at her home. We made friends quickly and laughed about what we were up to. I was extremely grateful. She pointed to the bathroom and smiled.

It was a big bathroom. When I entered I noticed it was basically four enormous cement walls. I saw a sink and a toilet but no shower. She did say shower, right? I knew it had to be there somewhere. I decided to get ready. Leaving my things by the door, I heard her say, "Lista?" I laughed, "As lista as I'll ever be!"

Moving quickly to where I thought a shower might go in this configuration, I looked up and noticed a few cracks in the walls. There was one big hole right in front of me. All of a sudden a gush of water hit me right in the face like a fire hydrant. My head bobbed back and forth with the sheer strength of the current. I was shocked and started laughing out loud, very loud. I heard the lady laughing too. She could have probably warned me but it was much more fun this way. She was having a good time herself. I learned that you just never know where God's blessings or provision will come. You simply need to trust and be Lista!

My Journal:
October 11, 1997

Precious Lord Jesus,

Here I am once again. I am 27 now and things have not changed. I need you right now like I needed you when I was 17 and when I was 7.

You are my very best friend Lord Jesus. Thank you for walking with me all through this life's journey. Thank you for constantly teaching me. Thank you for "growing me up" in so many ways and through so many circumstances.

So what's next, Lord?

It seemed that every three years or so I was put on a shelf. It was exactly how I felt before going to Ecuador. I knew there was more but I couldn't quite put my finger on it. Then, just before my shelf life ran out, there would always be some new direction. It was a test. Am I looking for what God has next or am I just trying to make something happen on my own? I had to wrestle that out many times and then once again get back to the main thing... following.

Typically I would fast one to three days depending on the situation. If I needed a breakthrough it was three days.

If I needed a fresh anointing and a word it was usually one day. When I took the time to seek the Lord and dig into the word there was always a "next step" visibly out in front of me. It was like a magic pathway that only got illuminated through seeking the Lord and waiting on his timing.

So what's next, Lord? While praying I decided to meet with my pastor, Don Foster, and get his counsel. He knew my story well. I shared some of my dreams and aspirations, explaining the crossroad I had come to once again. I had gotten a "normal" job at a jewelry store in the mall and was plugging away at being faithful in the little things; but, there was this sense that God had more and I was not content with average. Pastor Foster prayed with me and then looking up said, "I think you need to do a record of your own. I know a fellow you can call who works in music. He's in Nashville. Why don't you call him? His name is Michael Mellett. That's Pastor Ray Mellett's brother." I knew Michael. We had met in VBS at that same church when we were kids. He was probably making an eagle out of blown out matches while I was finger painting. Well, you have to consider, he was 12 at the time and I was only 8. Our families were actually good friends.

His brother Ray had been the associate pastor at that church for a number of years and had helped my dad and brother during the hardest times of Kieran's paralyzing accident. Ray's wife Debbie had tried to set Michael and me up from the time I was 16; but, Michael was now off becoming the next Christian artist and I was trying desperately to be the next Elizabeth Elliott. We weren't on the same page, not even close. Many times Debbie would call and invite me over because Michael was visiting from college. I felt flattered that she would call; I loved the family; I always had a great time with them. They were tremendously funny! I was guaranteed some serious laughter. I would go sing a few songs with Michael at the piano, catch up on what was going on, and basically say "Have a nice life" as I stepped out the door. No attraction. No curiosity. No consideration. It was platonic... as platonic as could be – not just for me, but for the both of us. He was pursuing other things. We were very focused.

I took my pastor's advice and called Michael. He kindly offered his help and encouraged me to visit Nashville to check out the possibilities of doing a record. So I went. During my visit, he allowed me to stay at his apartment while he stayed at a friend's house. That was typical of Michael, a gentleman to the core. I felt very comfortable around him. There was never any pretense. He was sincere; and, he loved the Lord just as much as I did. We spoke the same language when it came to our faith.

I showed Michael my songs and he liked what I was doing. As we were worshipping the Lord one day we wrote a song together and called it Sweet Surrender. Michael shared my love for the Spanish language although he was not bilingual. It was his favorite subject in high school and he had been on a mission's trip to Mexico. So we decided to translate the song. It was perfect. I felt like we were really getting somewhere. Now all I needed were the funds to get the recording done. A limited custom project could easily cost $10 thousand; that was cheap even years ago.

I returned home hopeful of what was to come. I started meeting with banks to see what kind of loans were out there. I considered doing fundraisers and headed down the road of finally doing my own project. I sensed God was in it. This whole process was awakening me to the possibilities of a greater ministry, a greater audience, and much more opportunity. I had sung on at least 15 records by now. I even wrote some recorded songs but never had my own project. This sounded very hopeful indeed.

One evening while I was praying the phone rang. It was Michael. He had some big news. He was called to go out on a world tour with Billy Joel. He was hesitant about it at first but then after much prayer, fasting, and a good heart–to-heart with his pastor, the Lord had made it clear he was to go. It was like his own mission field and he was asking for prayer. It was a Wednesday. He was scheduled to fly out for Japan that Friday. This of course meant that he would not be producing my record. I remember throwing my hands up in the air in disappointment to God; but, all I could do was encourage him. I even gave Michael Psalm 91 and he said that it was a confirmation – it was exactly what the Lord had given him. I thought, "Oh great, I'm even confirming this." Yes, I was glad for him but at the same time it felt like all the air was let out of my precious balloon. Stink!

Michael suggested another producer but the truth was that I couldn't pull my finances together. It was harder than I thought. No bank was willing to take the risk. I was back on the shelf; and, Michael was globetrotting.

I wasn't about self-promotion. Divine direction would be the only answer. I was pursuing the call. I had asked God at age 15 if he wanted to use my life and he said *yes*. That call didn't go away with my feelings. The call was alive and well, even if I was working in a jewelry store at the mall doing what seemed average to cover my needs. Faithful in the little things, I recollected. Don't despise the day of small beginnings.

I sang at Christian coffee shops, helped lead youth group, sang with the church worship team, and stayed faithful with whatever was before me. I even began dreaming of constructing my own abstinence program. This of course was while many of my friends were getting married and moving on with their lives. Tricky!

By this time Michael had been circling the planet, staying in five-star hotels, and keeping me informed on how to pray. By February of 1998 he had made his way to New York and asked if I would come to the Valentine's Day concert. His only motive was to let me get a bird's eye view of what this had been like for him, and to see what I had been praying for. I was thrilled and decided to bring a date. Yes, a date.   I remember getting ready to leave my parents' house with my date and hearing my father gently suggest that I guard my heart. Of course! This was just the only eligible bachelor in the whole stinkin' church at the time, but sure! Not so easy. I dated him for almost a year.

During that time, Michael would call to check up on me and stay in touch. Once he called me at "my date's" home. I remember feeling unbelievably uncomfortable. It was truly awkward. I knew I was settling. Michael was such a godly man. His voice alone brought me conviction. I recall hanging up and saying to myself, "I gotta get out of this." And so I did.

Recovering from that relationship was hardcore. I beat myself up for a number of reasons. I had to cut through some heavy duty soul-ties and once again come to grips with my original design, what I was made for. The question that kept lingering was whether or not I had missed it. Was this now plan B? How foolish! How could I have gotten so far off the beaten path? I'm sure other people were asking the same question. Self doubt, guilt and condemnation lurked around like my sidekicks. I needed to move past this but I didn't quite know how.

Sitting in my car by the lake near church one afternoon, I opened my Bible to a familiar verse, 1 Chronicles 17:25-27, "You, my God, have revealed to your servant that you will build a house for him. So your servant has found courage to pray to you. O Lord, you are God! You have promised these good things to your servant. Now you have been pleased to bless the house of your servant, that it may continue forever in your sight; for you, Oh Lord, have blessed it, and it will be blessed forever." I slammed my Bible shut, "No Lord. I'm not worthy of this. I'm not worthy anymore. I screwed up too much."

A thundering response resounded in my spirit, "WHO are YOU to say? This is not about YOU. This is about what I did. You need to forgive yourself. I already did. Humble yourself and accept my words."

Yikes! He was right. It was true. My pride had held me at bay. I needed to forgive myself. I needed to take him at his word, a word I had underlined in 1992. I heard it so clearly in my spirit as a missionary living on $75 a month. God very emphatically had declared that he was going to build me a house. He promised. It was done. I keeled over on my Bible; and, with a burst of tears, let forgiveness wash through my broken heart. This was not about me. It would never be about me. It was because of Jesus and what he had already done. My job was to accept the grace.

Pearl Power

God's gifts and his calling are irrevocable. God will not forsake us. He doesn't take back any promises. He's never working with plan B. He's working all things together as we yield our lives to him. It's outrageous but true. Oh the scandal of grace. "If we are faithless he will remain faithful, for he can not disown himself" —II Timothy 2:13.

God's Economy

Up to this point I had been living with others, paying for room and board. I really didn't know what it would be like to get out solo, to live on my own... all alone. That didn't sound very attractive, but it was necessary. There were some aspects of character and growth that could only be plowed through the land of "on my own." Where I lived there were no buses or cheap taxis, no sweet "empleadas" to help with the laundry; everything was at a distance. Rent, car insurance, groceries, electric, water, medical coverage, dental needs, and other basic necessities were in a "not so sure how all this goes" file in my head. I had paid for things, I had covered my expenses, always had a job since high school, even paid for some of my college studies, but the day-in-day-out "take care of it all" was new to me.

I didn't realize that this was just as important to God as my next ministry engagement. I needed a good dose of reality. God was trying to set me up to win. He knew I would have to grow in every area of life and he provided lots of opportunities for me to learn. Lots!

I had been renting a room from my friends George and Sylvia, a dear couple from church who lived on an enormous 2,000 acre estate. They were the caretakers. I felt spoiled having that time with them but got this feeling things were about to shift. It was a Friday morning and I heard it clearly in my spirit.

"Let go of the job Fiona."

"What? Remember, the job is what pays the bills?!"

"Let go of the job."

I had just moved out of my folks home six months prior and was trying to fly semi-solo. Being fully aware of the bills I now carried, I was surprised God would say such a thing; but, it was as clear as day. So, I let go of the job. My boss was very kind about the whole thing and asked what was next. "Uh oh," I thought. I really don't know what to tell her. "Something more," I responded, "More than I can say right now!" And off I went.

Saturday was interesting, as I was trying to figure out what this was all about. Sunday came and once again the Lord tested me.

"Put all your money in the offering plate."

"You do realize you just told me to let go of the job?" I responded softly. "That money is what I was hoping to use for the bills, Lord."

"Write the check."

"For all of it?"

"Yes."

"That's five hundred dollars, Lord?"

"Yes, put it in plate."

Oh for heaven's sake! This was a bit crazy; but, it was all too clear. My spirit was fully aware – it was God. He was asking for it all. I had learned not to withhold myself or anything I owned from the Lord. I wrote the check and truly felt joyful. It seemed ridiculous but it was really happening. As the plate came by I laughed out loud and then literally waved goodbye to the check in disbelief. Well, I guess I'm starting a fast, considering all my money is now in the offering plate. Lol!

Monday came and I decided to go up to the lake on the estate and talk to God. Yes, I was fasting alright. All I got was peace.

Pearl Power

It's the most unusual thing to experience deep peace that covers all your thoughts and feelings when in the natural you should be freaking out. How can you argue with peace? It doesn't lie.

That afternoon I got a call from a friend, Carollee. She heard that there was a job available at a Better Homes and Gardens real estate office and had offered them my name. Wow! That sounded great! I called the next day, had an interview, and was hired. This time I was making almost three times the salary with medical benefits and would be working on Main Street – a quaint historic town loaded with character and beauty. Okay!!!!

The truth was that I really didn't understand how much it would cost me to get an apartment and fly completely solo. But God did! He was setting me up for great things. Shortly after, I found the most adorable peach-colored stucco English cottage for rent out in the hills of my hometown. It was located in a summer resort area but amazingly affordable. God again!

When I moved in, I was just hoping to at least have a bed from home. My mom heard about a dear friend from the town garden club whose mother had passed away a year previous leaving a home full of antiques and fine furniture. She asked if I'd like to swing by and check it out. By the time we left I had a French Provincial dresser, long raw silk curtains, elegant gold-framed vintage prints, an enormous green cut velvet Irish down couch, a hand-carved Chinese ivory coffee table, two seats that matched, hand-carved wooden end tables, and a metal pot holder with the 12 tribes of Israel from the Holy Land. Oh God, you are outrageous!

My mother and her friend, Vora, were both extremely generous. They had worked out some deals and I was the humble recipient. Humble and grateful!

I loved my new place, my new job, and my new-found freedom. My boss, Ellen, really understood me. She was a delight and showed infinite amounts of patience as I learned the ropes in the office. There were a little over 30 agents, mostly women, all with different personalities. This provided limitless opportunities for growth and maturity. I was becoming!

TWELVE

An Unexpected Call

"For I know the plans I have for you, declares the Lord,
plans to prosper you and not to harm you, plans to give you
hope and a future. Then you will call upon me, and come
and pray to me, and I will listen to you. You will seek me
and you will find me when you seek me with all your heart.
I will be found by you, declares the Lord."
—Jeremiah 29:11-14a

Shortly after I walked into this new season I began to
seek God once again about my future. Even though I loved
my job I knew there was more. The nations were still calling. I decided to fast one day a week about my future, not
my husband or the children. I prayed specifically for my
future ministry. I was now 28 and believed with my whole
heart that God still wanted to use my life. Once again I was
responding to the call. With or without a husband I would
follow the call of God on my life. My question now was,
"Peru or Bolivia, Lord?" I had seen so much need and loved
the people dearly. I figured I could help in one of those
places. I had the language down and could minister quite
effectively. This time I had narrowed it down to these two
countries. Surely, it was Peru or Bolivia.

After fasting one day a week for six months, I received
an unusual call. It was Michael Mellett, my friend who was
going to produce my record but ended up on a world tour

with Billy Joel. The tour had ended and he had an invitation to Billy's 50th birthday party in New York. The invitation read *Michael Mellett and Guest*. He was calling to ask if I would be his guest. I thought that sounded very nice and told him I would pray about it. He was grateful for my response and said he would look forward to my call.

After we hung up, I called my folks. The conversation went like this:

"Hi, Michael Mellett just called and asked if I'd like to go to Billy Joel's 50th birthday party out on Long Island."

"MICHAEL MELLETT? GO!"

"You didn't even pray about it?"

"Michael Mellett? We don't need to pray about this one. You should go Fiona."

"Okay, you two, I'll pray."

It was pretty cool that their response had nothing to do with Billy and everything to do with Michael. But still, I knew somebody needed to pray. I prayed and I had peace. Peace means *go*! I called Michael and confirmed. He loved that I didn't say *yes* too quickly and respected that I wanted to check in with God first. I wasn't willing to take "whatever" seemed like a good opportunity. That week I would be turning 29, and I wasn't playing games now. I would have to hear from God or it would just be another distraction. My birthday was April 27th and the party was set for May 8th. This was imminent.

My "Esther Moment"

So, what does one wear to Billy Joel's birthday party anyway? The invitation didn't say. I started praying about that too. I wanted to represent Michael well. He had been such a faithful witness those two years and I really wanted to be a blessing to him. As I prayed I felt like the Lord was saying to get a new outfit. Then he said to get new shoes, then new jewelry, then new makeup. It seemed more like a makeover! You're probably thinking, "Of course he did. You like to shop!" Nope, actually not true. I'm not crazy about scouring clothing racks or walking through shopping malls for hours. I really don't like a million options. Being the frugal type, I was pretty shocked that he would tell me very plainly to buy all these things down to the makeup. I didn't feel like it was about hunting for the deals either. I was simply supposed to look great! Now that I look back, it was my Esther-moment and I didn't even know it. God was helping to put me together!

The next day I shared my upcoming event with the ladies in the agency. It was quite the buzz. They encouraged me to run down to some boutiques along Main Street. During lunch break I would try something on and run back to the office to show them. Fun! Some of them commented that I should get something sexier but I knew I needed to feel comfortable and be myself. I wasn't trying to impress anyone. I just wanted to be beautiful.

One day I found a gorgeous pantsuit (Yes, that was popular at the time, ha!). The pantsuit had dark grayish-blue crinkled material with very large satin lapels. I felt glamorous yet free. I didn't want to be distracted by my own outfit or overly self-conscious. This was perfect. It complimented my hair and eyes well. It was from a boutique; so, I knew I would be the only one wearing it. I didn't need everyone else's opinion. I could be content in my own comfort and style. Now on to shoes, makeup, and jewelry. Macy's was calling. I had never bought "professional makeup" before. I didn't even know where to start; but, I figured I'd find it all at Macy's. I was right. It was actually a lot of fun! I got to sit in one of those high chairs while someone else fussed over my coloring. They tried out a variety of colors on my eyes, cheeks, and lips until we were satisfied. I was looking good!

When it came to jewelry, once again I was drawn to the pearls; so, I just went with it. Pearl choker and pearl earrings to match my pearl ring and I was good to go! I was *God's Pearl Girl* on another mission. This one would change the course of my life

Pearl Power

God loves being the one to usher a woman into her Esther-moment. He loves to help make her look amazing; but, more than her outer garments or adornment, he loves to form her heart in such a way that it is the most attractive attribute she carries. She stands out in a crowd not because of her model-like walk, or her eloquent words, but the outrageous beauty that comes from a heart that is complete in Christ. She is secure, confident, and unashamed. She is *God's Pearl Girl!*

Billy Joel's 50th Birthday Party

From My Journal:
May 8, 1999

Dear Lord Jesus,

I offer up my life to you today. So many distractions... shoes, makeup, jewelry, hair. Oh Lord, let me be more concerned about my spirit and drawing close to you. Please quiet my spirit. Help me put my eyes fully on you, to offer every single detail up to you.

I pray for an intercessor's heart. I pray you would please heal me from this cold. Lord, I pray that I wouldn't be so concerned about what I look like or how I feel but that I would be in tune with your Spirit and flow with you.

Your Fiona

Two weeks came upon me quickly. Before I knew it May 8th had arrived. Michael pulled up in a fire red, brand spanking new mustang. He was ready! I, on the other hand, had my hair in a ponytail and was sniffling. The water heater had broken at my house, the water was shut off temporarily, I had a cold, and I wasn't even able to take a shower! Since this was Michael Mellett and we were friends and I wasn't trying to impress him, there was no pressure. I just told him about my situation and he, in his very easy-going and solution-oriented thinking, told me I could get ready in his room at the hotel Billy had rented for his guests. It was just a few miles from Billy's home in the Hamptons. I gathered all my makeover purchases and off we went. As we pulled away, Michael prayed that I would feel better; he blessed our trip and time together. We prayed that God would use us in powerful ways and that Jesus' light would shine brightly. It was a two-hour drive down to Long Island so he stopped and bought all kinds of provisions – all the most important things on a trip of this nature: M&Ms,

chips, café coolatas, and more chocolate. I started to feel better! Ha!

After getting ready, Michael told me I looked beautiful. I knew he meant it. I really did feel beautiful. The hotel attendant even complimented us on our way out and asked to take our picture.

This wasn't the first time someone had asked to take our picture: Once, four years earlier, we were meeting in New York City to discuss working on my music project and Michael was singing at the Waldorf Astoria; so, we took advantage of his trip and met to talk business. Afterward, we decided to take a walk through the famous Rockefeller Center. It was Christmastime and we were walking through four rows of 10-foot tall gold angels with trumpets when a guy selling Yankee baseball caps asked if we'd like our picture taken. We said *sure, why not* and then he asked if we were on our honeymoon. Huh? We assured him we were not married and laughed it off. Ha ha ha!

Now we were all dressed up and headed down this beautiful lane to Billy's home. It was a small road with high hedges – very much like Ireland. The sky was overcast, spraying a mist. All of a sudden we noticed a few men on the road with trench coats motioning for us to turn into a small entryway. It was a very basic gate with a security panel. They asked for our names and driver's licenses and then motioned for us to continue. We drove down a ways before getting to what looked like a clearing in a field. I saw a large home to one side but realized that must have been the guesthouse because the $40 million mansion could be seen in the distance. On either side of the lane, tucked into the grass, were old vintage sailboats. This brought new meaning to the words *yard decorations*.

On both sides of the home were courtyards, sculptures, and fountains. It was breathtaking. One enormous fountain was perfectly placed in the center of the yellow pebble driveway at the main entrance. Ten servants dressed in tuxedos lined the sides of the doors, complete with white gloves. We looked at each other, smiled in amazement, and said, "Well, here we go!"

The whole experience was quite surreal. As we walked through the home toward the party tent, we noticed gifts lining the hallway: Harley Davidson motorcycles with red bows, elaborate paintings, sailboat sculptures, and many large beautifully wrapped boxes. Michael had bought Billy a replica of a particular ship he loved and I wrote Billy a song. Yes, it's what came to me as I was praying for him that morning. I was tentative about it; but, when I prayed, it was all too clear. I checked with Michael first and then carefully wrote it on my card. It took a bit of courage but I did it. I don't remember the melody but this is what I wrote...

From My Journal:
May 8, 1999

Song for Billy Joel's 50th Birthday

"Waves in the Night"

Endless your grace, your touch and deepest peace
Perfect your love, pouring over me, sweetest embrace

And I feel your presence wash over my heart
Roll over my life
Like waves in the night

And although I cannot see you
I know you are rolling, rolling still
Faithful and true
You have held onto me
Like waves in the night, faithful are you

As a child my greatest memories
Were running on the beach careless and free
Looking over time I pray I always return to this place
Where I know my freedom is in you

And I feel your presence wash over my heart
Roll over my life
Like waves in the night
And although I cannot see
I know you are rolling, rolling still
Faithful and true
You have held onto me
Like waves in the night, faithful are you

And in the morning, at the break of day
When the sun comes up I can see once again
It's your mercy and your faithfulness
Rolling through me without end

Attached to Billy's home was a tent that accommodated the 400 or more guests. It was lined with elaborate material, bustled into varying elevations as if they were drapes at a grand theatre. There were gigantic urns filled with hundreds of garlic cloves and lemons as well as a variety of other fresh fruits and vegetables. This of course was just for decoration. A 30-member orchestra with the original singer from *The Godfather* soundtrack sat up on a platform behind the dance floor and the entire tent had parquet flooring. It was extraordinary!

We waited behind Billy as he was finishing up a conversation with his mother. Before Michael had a chance to say anything Billy turned around and gave me a big hug. He loves redheads! Favor! Michael simply laughed and pretended he was the stranger introducing himself. There was an ease and grace with being unpretentious. I had nothing to prove, no one to impress, and no agenda. We had a blast! It was like being at one of my cousin's weddings. We enjoyed our seven-course meal, many interesting conversations, took a tour of the house, even danced beside Christy Brinkley. She was the only person I recognized until Michael pointed out some of the people and gave names. While out on the dance floor, Liberty Devito, Billy's drummer, motioned to dip me. He is a very lightweight individual and I thought it might work better for me to dip him instead, so I did. Paul Reiser, from *Mad About You*, and his wife were watching on. They got a real kick out of the un-expected dip. I could tell Michael was having just as much fun. He hadn't experienced this *Fiona* before. All our meet-ings had been meetings, this was just for fun!

Michael pointed out Kathleen Turner, a famous actress whom I remembered from *Jewel of the Nile*. While waiting for a ginger ale she walked up beside me. I turned and said, "Hello Kathleen." She scanned me over once looking for a name.

"Fiona! Fiona Delamere?!" I said, as if she should know. In her deep dramatic voice she asked what I had been up to, so I told her. "You know, same old." She smiled, intrigued by my vagueness. I think at one point she was trying to fig-ure out what movies I had been working on when Michael appeared.

"Good evening Kathleen." She scanned him too.

"Michael Mellett," I assured her.

"So, tomorrow being Mother's Day," unaware of her motherly status, I prompted "Will it be breakfast in bed?" Her eyes grew wide.

"Of course!"

"At least you can expect cereal." Michael added.

She grabbed him by the collar with all her Hollywood demure and stated, "I hate cereal."

"Hate cereal!" he reinforced with equal drama.

Then, with a sweeping motion, she bowed adding a deep "Good evening", as she stepped back as if the curtain was about to close. We were certainly entertained!

Michael turned in surprise, "What was that all about?" I shrugged my shoulders and told him I thought she might be wondering what movie I was working on. And we laughed! It was brilliant.

After walking about the grounds, taking in Billy's collec-tion of world instruments, his life-size bronze sculpture of the *Last Supper*, an extensive living room with three individual areas for recording on three separate grand pianos, a magnificent library rotunda, a fireworks show of the *Long Island Sound*, and admiring the general splendor, we were feeling quite privileged to have this honor. This was no ordinary event. It was a three-day party.

When it was cake time they rolled a 12-foot culinary masterpiece to the dance floor. There were ooos and aaahhs and singing and dancing to follow. Many times Michael and I caught eyes just sharing the awe. There was an understood "This is ridiculously amazing" going on throughout the evening.

Michael introduced me to a very nice, tall man named Phil Ramone. I smiled and gave him a big hug. He was like a teddy bear. It was only later that Michael filled me in on who was who. That was when I learned that Phil had produced Mariah Carey and a number of other amazing artists. I loved not knowing because it gave me the freedom to simply love people and connect with them as people. I was respectful, but definitely gave a lot of hugs. People need hugs.

Michael and I sat and talked about the dream that was taking place around us, trying to recall the details for family and friends. By this time the tent had cleared and there was no one on the dance floor; but, the orchestra continued playing as if we were in Carnegie Hall. It reminded me of the movie *Sabrina*. The music was slow, soft, and floating through the air like expensive perfume. I thought for a second, "What a waste," and then decided to ask Michael if he would like to dance. He was slightly taken aback knowing it was slow and this would be a bit more vulnerable, but he gladly obliged. The musicians nodded and smiled as we braved the dance floor. With one hand on his shoulder and the other in his palm, I closed my eyes as we found our rhythm. I was unusually comfortable, the music was so beautiful, I felt slightly lost in it. I really didn't want to open my eyes but suddenly remembered a large tent pole being located somewhere in the middle of the dance floor and hoped we weren't going to hit it. I whispered, "Are your eyes open?"

"Oh, there's the pole" he said calmly.

And that's when I realized he was just as comfortable as I was and was thinking the same thing with eyes closed as well. At the end of the song we clapped for the band and decided to call it a day! What a day!

The Vision

On our drive home we marveled at the "God-moments" in the midst of all the pomp and circumstance. One of the band members had said to me, "Michael Mellett is such a good guy. I could never be like him." "Yes, you can!" I retorted. "What Michael has is a God-thing. Jesus did this. Sometimes we're holding on to what is fake because that's all we know. It's like holding on to fake plastic pink pearls when God's got the real thing. Mikimoto. We have to let go of what is fake to take hold of what is real. That's what Michael did. God can do it for you too. That's real life." He shook his head, but the truth was there. It was a seed. And that's all he needed to get started. We worshipped the Lord for a mission well accomplished at the party and on the tours. We had enjoyed ourselves tremendously and knew God had enabled us to be salt and light.

As we prayed and worshipped driving down the highway, the Holy Spirit flooded the car. The Bible says *draw near to God and he will draw near to you*. That's exactly how we felt. It was very sweet and very peaceful. Then something happened that was truly supernatural. It was as if a flat screen TV dropped in front of me out of nowhere and opened like a curtain six inches from my face. It was probably two feet wide. I could see Michael and me leading worship with a big band in front of thousands of people in Ireland. It looked like an auditorium and there was a large blue curtain in the back. I can't tell you how or why I knew it was Ireland, but I knew it was. I don't remember if God said that to me because I was really freaked out, to say the least! And then it closed. I turned at an angle toward my window and under my breath whispered, "GOD! What am I doing leading worship with Michael Mellett… in Ireland?!!!" No answer. I tried to act casual and decided that was something I would keep to myself. I would not tell a soul.

When we arrived at my house, Michael seemed more inquisitive about where I lived and what my life was all about. I invited him in to my peach stucco cottage and showed him all the beautiful things the Lord had provided. I even boasted of making my own honey butter, which he insisted on trying and was quite impressed. He told me he would be returning in a couple of weeks with some friends to New York City and would keep in touch. Then off he went in his fire red mustang!

What a day!!! I was on overload. If it were only the party to consider, that would have been enough information to last me a few weeks, but then on top of it, a vision. A REAL vision. I honestly didn't know what to make of it. I didn't want to make anything of it because I couldn't quite get my head around the whole thing. I had known Michael since I was eight years old. He was a *really nice guy*. We were not attracted to each other. He was going to be the next Michael W. Smith and I was going to be the next Elizabeth Elliott. It didn't compute. Yes, I felt comfortable around him but there was not even a hint of flirtation. This was different. So I decided to put it all aside, keep my eyes on

Jesus and seek him for what comes next. "Peru or Bolivia, Lord?"

The next day Michael called to reflect on the whole experience once again. It was so much to absorb in such a short time. Since we shared the experience it only made sense to talk about it all and remind each other of the details. There was a fresh depth of awe and gratitude and it made me realize how much I had truly enjoyed his company. What a great friend. It was good to connect.

Pearl Power

It is a great asset to a relationship when there has been a true friendship established outside of the realm of emotions and the unstable game of flirting. When there is no agenda other than kindness. Flirting is not sincere. It's like the sarcasm of romance. It's hard to get a proper read on a relationship when games are played. Love must be sincere or it just ain't love... not God's love, brotherly love, or romantic love!

Peru, Bolivia or NASHVILLE?

While praying one day, I started getting this funny feeling that I should check out Nashville. "Nashville, Lord? What's in Nashville?" Sure Michael was there and most of the Christian Music industry but I was looking for ministry, straight up ministry. I thought I would mention it to Michael when he came back up.

A few weeks later Michael came to New York City, but he didn't call. He was going to be at the famous *Four Seasons Hotel* for a special concert that Friday. When he didn't call that week I made a doctor's appointment and started to fill up my schedule. I was not going to sit around twirling my thumbs waiting for an invitation. I was a bit miffed. "Hmm? I thought we were friends? He said he would call." Nada.

By Friday I was slightly ticked but there was no way on earth I would call him. Besides, now I was too busy. Ha! I had to work till 5:00pm, go to the doctor's appointment, and stop by at my folks to connect with family. I had places to go, people to see, important stuff to do, whatever it was. I would never make it there on time anyway! Even if I did have an invitation, which I DIDN'T. But I was OK with that!!! "Have a nice time with your 'friends,' MICHAEL MELLETT!!"

There had been some construction going on next door to my office, loud banging and obnoxious drilling. "Can you even think with this noise?" my boss said as she rounded the corner to my desk.

"Oh sure!" I'm just FINE!"

"Why don't you leave early?" she asked.

"Oh no, that's okay."

"I insist. I can't take it and I won't leave you here either. Please leave early."

"Okay?" I bemoaned.

Then the phone rang. It was my doctor's office. "We are so sorry but we will have to reschedule your appointment."

"What?" What's going on, God?"

So I went to my parents' house. No one was there. So much for places to go and people to see! I decided to call my home and get my answering machine messages. I hear, "Hi Fiona. It's Ray Mellett (Michael's brother). Michael is in New York City. You should give him a call. If you were thinking at all of calling him it would be a really good idea." Click. "No, no I shouldn't. I'm not thinking of calling him," I say to myself and hang up.

In walks my little sister Deirdre. She is 12 years younger than I am, 17 at the time. She listens to my story quite attentively. I explain how I shouldn't call and I don't even have anything to wear and I wouldn't go by myself.

She smiles and says, "You should call. I'll go with you. Here's a dress." She's five feet tall mind you. The dress fit perfectly.

"Hey Michael. Ray called and said I should call you?"

"Meet you at the Four Seasons Hotel?"

"Sure, I've got nothing else going on…"

"Yes, Deirdre can come with me."

"Okay, see you then."

WHAT? How did that happen? Can I still be mad? I guess that's over now. I'm going to New York City with my little sis!

Oh the drama of the female species and the complete recovery of it all. Under the right set of circumstances she is more than capable of pulling off the miraculous. Crying one moment, and laughing the next. She can perform a complete makeover in less than five minutes and walk out in high heels as if nothing, absolutely nothing, has fazed her. Grace at its finest was lifting me up and helping me get over myself and out the door. It was a divine appointment. All of heaven must have been cheering as it took a few hundred angels to get me going in the right direction. My prince was waiting. As my future father-in-law said so eloquently to my future mother-in-law the very first moment they met, "This thing is bigger than the two of us, baby." It was certainly bigger than Michael and me.

From my hometown to Manhattan it's typically just under an hour ride. We jumped into my little black, two-door Mercedes coupe diesel, the nicest hand-me-down I ever got. It wasn't long before we could see all the city lights. I marveled at how the Lord had literally made it work. It was more than just a coincidence. Destiny was calling once again.

Deirdre and I thoroughly enjoyed ourselves. After the concert we headed to a diner with Michael and his best friend Kip. I broached the subject about checking out Nashville. Kip asked when I'd like to come. I asked if they were busy Memorial Day weekend a couple of weeks away. Kip quickly responded, "Whatever it is, we'll clear the schedule. Just come!" Michael looked over with surprise at his forthrightness and agreed. It was done. I would take a long weekend off and scope out the prospects of a move. Two weeks later I was on a flight to Nashville, Tennessee. My boss even told me to stay an extra day if need be. (What boss says that?)

Michael had bought a new home, a sweet little spot on the planet in the historic district. He filled all the flowerpots with fresh flowers and had painted the guestroom. He had great taste in art and décor, a collection of old cameras, vintage kitchen appliances, lots of chrome and muted colors, very masculine, and very Michael. He showed me around town, took me on walks, introduced me to his friends, and we worshipped the Lord on his Wurlitzer. We kept it all pretty light and open. When he dropped me off at the airport they said my flight had been canceled. I called him and before I knew it he was right behind me saying over my shoulder, "Same time, same station, tomorrow?"

"Yes." smiled the attendant.

I called my boss and for some reason she was not surprised.

The next day we had lunch with Michael's friends and one of them mentioned a job opening at the church. We stopped by to inquire. While filling out an application, the main administrator, McLauren, informed us that there was indeed no such position available. She then proceeded to ask if she could interview me anyway. That was surprisingly unexpected, considering she had just said there was nothing available. As I shared with her what I had been praying about she smiled softly and said, "I wish I did have a position for you here. I like you." The feeling was mutual. She was a kindred spirit, for sure.

Heading to the airport, this time with Kip in the front passenger's seat, he asked, "So, what are you going to do?"

"Well, I don't know. I guess I'll pray and see what's next?"

"You know exactly what to do," he responded emphatically.

"Well, I'm not sure."

"Yes, you do. You need to move here. It would be like a slap in God's face if you didn't."

Wow! That was pretty straightforward.

Kip didn't say a lot but when he did speak it always sounded like he had some extra information I was not privy to.

I just laughed and said, "OK?"

As I boarded the plane that day I didn't have any major answers but I did have a great sense of expectation. There was peace and a true sense of divine destiny behind all the details.

The very next day McLauren called from the church saying she didn't have a job available yesterday but she did have one today. Her very own assistant put in a two weeks' notice that morning.

"Huh?! Really? Okay!"

"Can we schedule a second interview and fly you down?" she asked.

"Um, sure!" I responded in disbelief.

What church flies a young lady in for a second interview as an assistant to the administrator? As if there weren't enough young ladies in Nashville to choose from. This was comical! No church does that kind of thing. I'm pretty sure God was just showing off. He's so fun!

When I returned to tell my boss about the possibilities, she was amazingly supportive. She knew there was more to the story. So did Esther, the office manager, an elderly Jewish woman. She came and sat by my desk.

"Talk to me about this Michael."

I gave her some background on our friendship, history, and what had ensued. She looked at me inquisitively; so, I repeated the part about us being *just friends*.

"Yes, you keep saying that," she replied.

She sat for a moment and then spoke a word I had never heard before, "Basherter!"

"I'm sorry?"

"Basherter, Basherter!"

"What does that mean?"

"It's Yiddish. An old Jewish word."

"Okay. But what does it mean?"

She leaned in, with a very resolved look and stated, "What is ordained of God is ordained of God."

My eyes grew wide.

"A match made in heaven," she says. She then stood up and walked away.

I sat in a daze wondering how that could be possible. It just didn't make a whole lot of sense. I was going to marry a pastor, evangelist, missionary or at least someone in ministry who spoke Spanish and was going around the world. But my spirit seemed very comfortable with the idea. Something was getting clearer on the inside. I really couldn't put it into words but something was in the works!

Pearl Power

You don't have to know all the details to follow God but you do have to trust him. Sometimes the next step doesn't show up until you stick your foot out. "Trust in the LORD with all your heart and do not lean on your own understanding; in all your ways acknowledge him, and he will make your path straight."
—Proverbs 3: 5-6

THIRTEEN

Interviews and Arrangements

"I, wisdom, dwell together with prudence;
I possess knowledge and discretion."
—Proverbs 8:12

On my second interview Michael decided to have me stay with his friend Prudy, which was short for Prudence. Yes, that was her name! And that was her place! She was wonderful. By this time I knew I couldn't be staying at Michael's place. It wasn't *prudent*. Even though we were not dating, not anything, it was better to keep some clean lines. *Avoid the appearance of evil*, is what the Word says. This was Michael's call. I agreed.

Surprise, surprise I got the job! Ha! Michael was working on a project at Amy Grant's house and had allowed me to borrow his car for the interview. I had to drop him off at Amy's and go pick him back up. What a hardship! This was a normal day in the life of Michael Mellett. He had graduated from Belmont University with a vocal production major and paid his dues waiting tables for six years as he made his way into the industry. Now he worked with all the top artists and played a major role in vocal production, contracting groups of professional singers to sing on recordings and coordinating BGVs (background vocals) for live recordings with major labels. Michael was sought after in his field not only for his talent, but also for his composure, diplomacy, and God-heart. He could calm any weary artist and bring the best out of them, as he always brought Jesus to the studio.

When Michael came to pick me up at Prudy's for church that Sunday, I was wearing a blue dress with pearls. As I came down the steps he said, "You look beautiful." No games, no flirting, just sincere. He said what he meant and meant what he said. I was beautiful- no strings attached, not looking for anything in return, just giving a compliment. I felt very respected and beautiful.

It was now the middle of June. I would move there in two weeks. Michael pulled out the newspaper that afternoon and started looking for an apartment. He circled an ad. The address showed it was just around the corner from his place. How convenient. We took a walk and found this gorgeous stone building. The apartment was perfect. I was very grateful for his help. He really cared.

Back in New York I jumped right into packing. While I was making plans, Michael called and said he would be up visiting family for a week and could help me move if I wanted the help. Want? Need was the word. Sure!

He and my sister Deirdre share a birthday, June 30th. When my sisters found out he was coming, they said we should all go swing dancing in New York City for Michael and Deirdre's birthdays. I invited him and he accepted. That day my sisters decided they wanted to go to the opera house instead. I was so embarrassed. It looked like I had set it up. I called my older brother Kieran to explain and he said, "Just go. Michael Mellett is a great guy. He won't think anything weird. Don't worry. Just go." So I did.

When I saw him I realized we were matchy, matchy. He was wearing khaki pants and a white shirt with a bold spring-green stripe across his chest. I was wearing khaki pants with a green shirt that matched his stripe. It was funny but slightly awkward at the same time. It looked like we had planned it, especially for swing dancing. All those people love to match. You can only imagine how hard God was working to give me a clue.

First we headed to Cara Mia, a quaint Italian Bistro off 46th Street. We tried to act like there was nothing going on but couldn't help trying to figure things out as we sat there in this romantic setting with blank stares and basic conversation. Just keep breathing, smile a little but not too much. Don't look too interested. Don't lead him on. I found myself criticizing little things and pointing out our differences in the back of my head. Every time I felt secure in my judgment the Holy Spirit would remind me of my own flaws. "He has a mole on his wrist." "You have chubby, square toes". "He is so Irish". "Did you forget your freckles?" "Oh, right."

We finished up at Cara Mia's and were on to the main attraction, Swing 46th just down the avenue where we would now assume a dancing position and pretend everything was just hunky dory. I really just wanted Michael to have a fun time for his birthday, make some memories, and be a good friend. What I didn't know was that he had been praying, seeking God and preparing his house to receive me for each visit. He was struggling, trying to trust God and trudging through his own personal criticisms and insecurities. His internal conversation was filled with questions, wondering if this was really God putting the pieces together, and asking for help.

At Swing 46th they start with an hour dance lesson, then bring out the live band from San Francisco and let you do your thing. We were the best in our class until all the professionals from Broadway showed up for the band. They were doing some major flipping and swinging!

The whole evening I was so restless. I would feel comfortable for one moment and then awkward the next. The dance motions were back and forth, close and far. That's about how I felt. I must have excused myself to go to the bathroom five times. No telling what Michael was thinking. But he was completely consistent, understanding, easy-going and so very nice, an absolute gentleman.

Afterward we took a stroll down to Howard Johnson's on Broadway for an old-fashioned ice cream experience. We sat at the long countertop, eating cones and trying desperately to act relaxed and nonchalant. In the back of my head I was thinking, "GOD, what is the DEAL???" By this time I had become an emotional ball of silly string. I felt like a complete yoyo. Something was going on and it was out of my control. I couldn't put my feelings and my discernment together. They didn't match. God was trying to help me but for some reason I was freaking out. I kept it cool on the outside (I think) but on the inside I couldn't pull it together. As I dropped him off at Grand Central Station he thanked me for our time together and hopped out of the car waving as he shut the door. I waved back and then said out loud, "GOD! I am NOT going to marry that man!" I think I was trying to be in control or pretend I could be for a moment. All the way home I swayed back and forth, reeling from the evening's rubber band effect on my mind and emotions. Finally I just had to let it go. There was nothing else to think. The only thing left was to trust.

Nashville Here I Come

As promised, a few days later Michael was at my house ready to take the long journey from New York to Tennessee. Something about letting go, starting fresh, following the leading of the Holy Spirit and having Michael by my side gave me this amazing peace and comfort. Back to peace and on my way. We made it as far as Virginia and found a hotel on a hill for the night, *The Wassail Inn*. Yes, I did notice all the billboards with hearts all over, "Virginia is for Lovers!" We parked and walked in the lobby. Michael asked the woman at the desk for two rooms. She looked up and said, "What? Y'all don't like one another?" He responded, "Yes, we like one another we just need two rooms." "We like one another; what is he saying?" I thought. "Oh, y'all are getting married, trying to do things right?"

"No, we just need two rooms."

"You can get a discount on one?"

"Two rooms please?"

I couldn't take it. Noticing all the wild animals that were stuffed and standing in the corner I blurted, "Did you shoot those bears yourself?" "I sure did," she said with a big smile. And we each got a room. No more questions.

Something was changing. We were both absolutely ourselves around each other. There was never any pretense. I felt very comfortable, like the time when we were dancing at Billy's party. Now it *all* started to seem like a dance. Instead of stepping on God's feet, I decided to go with the peace and not struggle internally. The rest of our trip was easy. We pulled into Nashville and it felt like home.

Pearl Power

God's plans for your life will surpass anything you can imagine. You can trust his ways and his thoughts. "For my thoughts are not your thoughts, neither are your ways my ways, declares the Lord. As the heavens are higher than the earth so are my ways higher than your ways and my thoughts than your thoughts" Isaiah 55: 8-9. It's like the difference between a paper airplane and a jumbo jet 747. If you choose to trust him implicitly you will be amazed!

Home is Where Your Heart Is

The first week in town Michael sent flowers to "welcome me home." He also gave me an unusual gift, a cell phone. He just wanted to make sure he could contact me anywhere at any given moment. Ha! What a very nice guy! Every day felt like light years in my heart. It was as if God was working with thousands of little strings to connect me to him. I didn't realize how independent I had grown as a single missionary and minister. I had been holding up so much for so long. God was now asking me to trust him in new ways. This took some work, but not too much. It was only two weeks into my new venture when we had "the talk."

I couldn't invest anymore unless I had an accurate account of my reality. If this was real I could move forward. My heart had now grown double in size for this man and I needed words. Michael clarified that he was indeed pursuing me. I had asked about my "status." He assured me I wasn't simply another good "female" friend. Then he smiled real big like he had explained it all. I smiled too and thought, "Huh, I think something is going on. Not quite sure what to call it but it's real, whatever it is." When he returned, he threw his arm around me as we sat on the couch. That's when I realized he had poured his heart out, gave me all his words. Typical male syndrome. Okay then. Michael later explained that he was not at liberty to pursue me while I was still distant because I had to make some decisions for myself. He could see some of where we were headed but couldn't see it all. He needed to trust God with getting me there and then take it in the rhythm God provided.

The next week I had a friend visiting from New York. Michael and I went to pick her up at the airport. While waiting at the gate I realized I didn't have specific words to explain this relationship to her. So I turned to Michael and said, "What should I tell Margie?" He looked around slightly dumbfounded. "I mean, how should I explain us to her?" He was still looking for the word, searching through certain categories in his head. I could see the concern. He thought he had explained it all and then realized I needed more words, a specific word. But what was it?

"An item... We're an... item."

"An item?!" All I could think of was some movie out of the '40s.

"Uuuuuhhh," he searched some more realizing this might not cut it.

I started to laugh, "An item?"

He laughed too. "We're together."

"Okay," I smiled. She would just have to figure it out on her own. And she did. He held my hand.

The Signs On Our Foreheads

Two weeks later I had to return to New York for my brother's graduation from chiropractic college. I asked Michael if he wanted to go and he went and bought our plane tickets. That would be a *yes*!

This man wanted to take care of me. He had waited for this for what seemed to be a lifetime. There was no mistaking. He was focused and ready! He was on it! I was ready too. I couldn't believe how much everything had turned around in such a short time. It reminded me of the scripture I would hang on to, "Do not awaken love until it so desires." Real love is God. God would have to awaken real love in me at his precise timing. One thing was clear, there was some serious "awakening" taking place!

Upon arrival in New York we had to make a five-hour drive with my parents up to the small town where the graduation was taking place. My parents were over the moon! Our conversation was filled with laughter, deep heart connection, godly fellowship, and sweet peace. We had so much in common it made all the communication flow like a river. There were no hiccups.

At one point I was reading my Bible. I had one of those zip-up Bible carriers and inside I kept a few precious treasures. All of a sudden an old paper slipped out from inside. Before I had a chance to grab it, Michael had already reached down. From the top of the list he read, "What I Would Like in a Husband" and said, "May I?" I was a bit dismayed but felt like it was too late to put it away. I nodded and held my breath as he read...

Just a List of What I Would Like in a Husband:

—a man who loves God with all of his heart, mind and strength

—a man who knows the Word of God like the back of his hand

—one who is confident of God's call on his life yet humble to allow God to direct him in whatever way

—a man who my father will respect and love and who my family can freely accept

—a man who is a virgin and who has been keeping himself pure

—a man who is musically talented and who will blend beautifully with my talents

—a man who will be the priest of my household and who has a heart for missions

—a man who can pick up a language easy or who is already bilingual

—I want a man of God who will be faithful to God first, his wife and family second, and his ministry third

—a man who can understand my culture, language, expressions and mannerisms for who I am Thank you Jesus!

—A man from a whole Christian family whose parents have a good wholesome marriage.

No one else had ever read my list. This was waaaaay personal. It was not the first draft I had written over the years but it was certainly the last. It had to be at least seven years old. He held it gently and in his mind checked off the list one by one. Finally he turned to me handing it back and smiled. We didn't say a word. He just held my hand a little tighter.

When we got to the hotel, Michael went to my brother's room; then I walked into the room I was staying in with my folks. My dad closed the door behind me. The two of them faced me with tears in their eyes saying in amazement, "Fiona, that's your husband!" My face was beaming, "You're right!" We laughed and cried and hugged tightly. It was a moment of awe and wonder. It was Michael Mellett all along. Who knew?

It dawned on me that every time I went to minister at an English-speaking church I had been ministering with Michael, my future husband. You see, I would take background tracks to sing popular Christian songs. These artists were all people Michael sang with and every time I used an original track Michael's name was on the jacket and you could hear his voice in the background. I had been singing with him for 10 years and only now put it all together. What a fantastic surprise!

On the way home it was all we could do to keep my father from talking about engagements and proposals. He couldn't help himself. We stopped to get a bite to eat and he just kept on going. As we sat in a booth at Roscoe's Diner off the Taconic State Parkway, Dad was smiling from ear to ear telling how he proposed to my mom when a gentle love-tap came from under the table. Well, it was actually a love-kick from my mom. She was sitting directly across from him. Desperate measures for desperate times. What a hoot! My mother had to stop him somehow. We joke about it now, saying he almost proposed to Michael. I would have been married that night if it were up to my dad! He's such a romantic... when God is in it, of course. Well, if you remember, it was already double the amount of dating time compared to when he had asked my mother. We had been dating two weeks already. He proposed in six days. Hilarious!

That evening at my parents' house, Michael stayed on the first floor. I was on the third. I said *good night* and he reached over and kissed me for the first time. It was very sweet and I felt the waves of "awakening."

He had asked me to speak to him in Spanish whenever possible. He wanted to learn and was truly inspired. So he said, "Bueno, ya nos fuimos a mi cama." I knew he had no idea what he was saying. Normally you would say "Well, it's time to go to bed." But he said, "Well, it's time for us to go to my bed." I giggled and said, "Buenas noches." He stood there smiling, wondering what the laugh was for as I turned to go upstairs. It wasn't until a few minutes later, as he reviewed his words, that it came to him – he roared laughing. Michael was so embarrassed. He thought about calling me but I was already on the third floor and he would just have to wait till tomorrow. We would need to work on that Spanish!

Pearl Power

Don't let a kiss pull you into a relationship, let the Holy Spirit do the pulling. If God's not drawing you in, it is best to run the other way. Your heart is not a playground. It's a garden. You don't need anyone stomping around in your garden. Don't settle for less. You don't have to.

We spent time with Michael's family and got the same response. Everyone could see the little signs written on our foreheads in heavenly gold letters "I'm for him" and "I'm for her." There was no explaining. It all made perfect sense. It was God! I was amazed because I had known this family since I was a child. I loved them already and now I was going to be a part of them.

When we were children, Michael and my sister Siobhan were penpals. They sat together at church when he visited. One day our families decided to go to a state park together. This was the day my sister decided she no longer wanted to be penpals with Michael. He was very disappointed. After learning the news, Michael came back to where his dad was, feeling dejected and forlorn. His dad quickly turned, looked at me, and said to Michael, "Why are you so concerned about that one? This is the one with all the fun." I'm pretty sure I was climbing a tree at that point, with no telling how much mud on my outfit; not to mention I was still trying to grow into a good set of front teeth. I don't think Michael was all that impressed at the moment; but, as God would ordain, his father passed away the following year. These were words Michael remembered clearly and now cherished more deeply than ever. His father saw something that day and he was right. I was the one!

Pearl Power

Your family and friends on a whole can tell when you are in the right relationship. That accountability is priceless. They will see things objectively. They can also tell when things don't completely line up. Remember, you're not just marrying the person; you're marrying the family... for life. It's important to have favor with a potential future family-in-law. Marriage is a great commitment that comes with hard work. The more you have in common the easier the flow. If it's a struggle before you get married it will be much harder later on. Do yourself a favor and be completely honest about your situation. Emotional involvement makes it difficult to see straight, physical involvement is blinding. You have to take a step back to actually see what you truly have. Waiting for God will prove to be the smartest choice ever. You WILL be blessed!

Basherte and Basherter

One day, while spending time with Michael's family, his mother brought up the word "basherte." I turned in surprise and asked her to repeat the word. The only other time I had heard this word was from Esther, the old Jewish woman at Better Homes & Gardens. She was the one who repeated the word over and over and then stood up declaring with conviction, "What is ordained of God is ordained of God. A match made in heaven." And then walked out. *Bashert* is Yiddish for "destiny" and is most commonly used in the context of one's divinely foreordained spouse, basherte (female) and basherter (male). Michael's mom, who has a great love for the Jewish people and the nation of Israel, said *basherte*, again explaining that many years ago she had watched a movie with Michael where they mentioned this word and ever since she had been praying for his *basherte*. My eyes got wide! What is ordained of God IS ordained of God!

On Your Mark, Get Set, Wait

It is an unusual situation when you know who you are going to marry, you've waited for him for what seemed to be a lifetime, and you've now been dating him for two weeks.

How is this supposed to go? Can I get engaged today and marry you tomorrow? What's the hold up? Ha! It feels like: "On your mark, get set, WAIT." I had to hit the brakes in my head and live in the moment, just like Elizabeth Elliot said. I needed to keep Jesus at the center; and, I needed to learn what it was to simply be loved. It didn't matter what we were doing as long as we were together. We tried to fit in as many breakfasts, lunches, and dinners as possible. We shared dreams, challenges, long walks, chocolate, and lots of coffee. There was a rhythm and a flow to growing in love and we were allowed to take our time. Michael made room for me in every area of his life and romanced me every chance he had. It was precious and all kinds of wonderful.

Pearl Power

Every pearl of truth I had acquired in my walk with Jesus was now the adornment I wore through our dating, courting and engagement experience. And it beautifully carried right into our marriage. Just because I found "the right one" didn't mean I could let my guard down and give myself away. I'm sure many people feel tempted to do that but the truth is that it's a test. Will you be faithful to God first? It builds trust to wait. Having a strong foundation would be worth the wait.

Three Little Words

It may have been a month after we started dating that I found myself in need of some more words. We laughed over the "item" conversation many times and then one night I realized I really did need more of an explanation.

Most of what we experienced was in actions and responses but now I needed WORDS.

I read that women typically use 30,000 words a day and men 10,000. Neither one of us were typical anything; but, I found it true that at the end of the day he might not have used up all his words, especially the important ones. So one evening I asked Michael for more words. I was just looking to hear a bit more of what was going on in that heart of his. Just a little. He took a moment to think about it and then, looking at me very seriously, he said, "Well, the truth is... I love you."

Woah!!!! Wasn't looking for THOSE words but I felt it. Deeply. He was not messing around. And he continued... quite emphatically... explaining his love and what that meant. I was still picking my jaw off the floor when he held my hands and said it again, "I love you!"

Alrighty then, *those are some WORDS*. I knew I couldn't just dish it back. I had to wait for my moment, but boy was I shocked. He really loved me. I could feel it. He wouldn't say it if he didn't mean it. He didn't play with words, ever. His love was sincere and I felt like the most wonderful woman on the planet. This was real.

Just Because

One day in mid September Michael called. "Tomorrow I would like to pick you up from work and take you out for a special evening. Please get dressed up." Well, okay then!

Michael showed up right on time wearing a suit and holding one single red rose. Hmm? "This looks like a big deal," I thought. "Special indeed!"

He brought me to The Melting Pot, a fondue restaurant, where we had everything from shrimp and filet mignon to pineapple and chocolate on skewers. It was great fun! Our table was in a remote area of the dining room. A very intimate setting where one might possibly be asked a special question? Was he going to ask me? Tonight? Seemed like a whole lot of "special" going on; and, then he asked for the check.

Okay, well, maybe not.

Then it was on to ride a horse and buggy.

"Okay, this must be it. Really? A horse and buggy?"

We rode all through downtown Nashville, hugging and kissing and enjoying our surroundings. It was the perfect night to get engaged on a buggy. Then, he helped me down and drove me home.

Really?

I felt so loved, so well taken care of, truly blessed but slightly confused. I was going through the details in my head, trying to work this out.

We got all dressed up.

He gave me a rose.

Brought me to a fancy restaurant, gushed the whole night through with how much he loved and appreciated me.

He took me on a horse and buggy ride and held my hand the whole time.

We gazed at stars, laughed and cried over God's goodness and were perfectly aware that we would be getting married.

And now he was dropping me off.

For a second I questioned, "All this for nothing?"

I'll never forget his words as he leaned over to kiss me good night.

"*Just because...*" There was a pause and then he explained, "I'm sure you were wondering what this was all about and I want to tell you that this is Just Because... Not for any special reason or purpose other than to say *I love you.*"

"Okay?" And then up I went to my apartment to discuss this in further detail with the Lord. Jesus and I needed to talk. I didn't know if I should laugh or cry I was so jumbled up. Finally it dawned on me that Michael was setting me up for a *marriage* and not just a *moment*. I had to learn how to give Michael the reins of leading this thing and let him romance me as he wanted to. This was his place, his role and I needed to give him some room to lead. It wasn't up to me when we would get engaged. This was a reality check. I started thanking the Lord for a wise and godly man. He would hear God very clearly and I would be very blessed.

"Just because" was alright with me!

Pearl Power

When the time is right let your man be the man. Let him pay, let him open the door, let him be the gentleman, and let him show that he will be responsible. Let him rise to the occasion. Wait in the car for him to open the door. Give him opportunities to lead. It's good for him. Have a healthy expectation of his character, show mutual respect, and make your boundary lines known very early. Use words that build him up and expect the same in return. Avoid sarcasm, mocking and empty flirtatious chatter. Don't put yourself in precarious situations. Avoid the appearance of evil. Don't hang out alone if you know you will be tempted to do the wrong thing. Think it through beforehand. He is to be head and shoulders above you spiritually so that you will respect him and eventually follow his leadership in the your home after marriage. He is still a man. Don't tempt him. Respect him. You are a powerful force in his life. Take good care of his heart.

Between March and May

After releasing all that to the Lord I sure did enjoy myself a lot more. It was different trusting God through someone else with my life. Trust indeed. I had to learn to trust Michael. There were layers to this. One thing I knew was that God wouldn't give me more than I could handle and if I needed a heads up he would provide. He was still my all in all, my everything, my God.

One morning in October I woke up, sat straight up in my bed, and said the words "between March and May" out loud. It was weird; but, I immediately knew I would get married between March and May. I said, "Thank you Lord! See, that's all I needed." And I laughed!

Later that day I told Michael about my "waking words." He smiled and said, "Yep, that's it. I felt like the Lord said December engagement, May wedding."

Woohoo! It was settled!

Studios and Spanish

I still loved to sing and minister but no one really knew me in Nashville. I would have to build my life once again, love God, love people, and let it come together naturally. It seemed like every three years I was shelved. I had phenomenal ministry moments, sang in concerts of 50,000 people or more, traveled the world, recorded with famous artists, was considered semi-famous in Latin American Christian music, and now that was on the shelf. Yet, I was okay. I didn't know what God would do but I knew he wasn't finished with me.

One day when Michael was recording in a studio I stood listening behind the producer, Bobby Shin. At one point I started singing without thinking where I was or what was going on. I was simply enjoying the worship music. It was anointed, so I joined unconsciously. Bobby turned around and looked at me and pointed to the studio. "You need to get in there."

"Oh no, that's okay."

"Yes, you need to get in there."

I knew I could sing but there's a difference between singing your heart out for Jesus and session-singing in Nashville. There are A singers, B singers, and then everybody else. I would have considered myself a B+ singer for vocal control, pitch, balance, and anything else someone might hear on any given moment in the studio. Anointing A +, singing B. Yes, I took lessons, practiced, and sang all over the place, but I didn't have the studio training. You can cover a whole lot in a concert. It doesn't need to be perfect and if the Holy Spirit is moving, you can do just about anything and it sounds great, ha! Well, maybe not anything but there's a flow.

Michael knew I could sing but he also knew he couldn't make a way for me in the studio. I would have to hold my own. I would have to polish it up myself, train my ear and be teachable. His ear was perfect. We called him the *parts police*. He could hear all my stuff. He could tell me what to do but what he couldn't do was make it happen for me. If I could hold my own in the studio I could sing with the big dogs. You either had it or you didn't. The studio wasn't the place to learn. You were called because you were a professional.

It was hard at first. I had potential but I wasn't exactly there. It was a risk for Michael to hire me on projects. He knew he couldn't cover for me. He might have to stop and guide me a bit. I had to listen very carefully, pull my pitch up, align myself to the other singers, blend my volume, and humble myself with a big smile after being corrected. At times I would get nervous because I would become self-conscious. It's normal to do retakes but I would get a little jumbled if I did a couple of retakes before getting a part. I had to learn what there was grace for, what was normal studio life was, and how to control being nervous or emotional. It was mainly internal but sometimes I leaked. I knew most of the time when I was slightly off. But if I was caught off guard I would feel bad; and, the harder I tried, the more I would screw up. So, I would have to relax and talk myself off my little ledge. The last thing I wanted to do was embarrass Michael. I loved making him proud. I wanted to be my best.

In the same way, Michael had asked me to teach him Spanish. I was bilingual and he wanted to be the same. We practiced constantly from the moment we started dating. Whenever we found ourselves with Latinos he would use everything he could remember. Sometimes it came out great, other times, like at my folk's house, he would say it wrong and be slightly embarrassed. I would guide him through longer conversations and every day he expanded his vocabulary. He was determined to learn Spanish and I was determined to learn the studio.

One day, after Michael realized I could really hold my own in the studio, he decided to talk a little more about what our future held. He said I would probably need to let go of my job and that he wanted me to just take the jobs God provided in the studio and in ministry. He was thinking about travel, live recordings, and ministry. All I could think of was being a stay-at-home wife and having my independence pulled out from underneath me. And I said as much. He was surprised at my reaction and the amount of emotions that followed. Man, letting go of singleness, and trusting this man was no joke. I didn't get a heads up from God this time; so, I was a bit raw. He decided to leave that particular subject alone for a bit. Smart man!

Pearl Power

Learning to trust God is one thing. Learning to trust God through someone else is another. It takes double the trust and a daily dose of fresh grace. Even though God brings people together it is never to take away from personal devotion to Jesus. We find out quickly how unrealistic our expectations can be and that no one can take God's place. Jesus must be first for the rest to work. The key is still getting to him each morning before the day gets away and keeping him at the center of it all.

FOURTEEN

December to May

"You will be like a well-watered garden, like a
spring whose waters never fail."
Isaiah 58:11

He said December engagement but he didn't say when
in December. It could be the first or the thirty-first. Here we
go again. I was hoping it would NOT be a New Year's Eve
engagement. I feared that I might slap him instead of giving
my consent. Well, come on, he gave me some information
and then left it up to my imagination. Every day I would be
wondering if this was it. It sure was a faith journey. One
thing I knew was that I could trust Jesus in him. Yes, I could
trust him but above that I could trust God working through
him and this was merely the beginning!

Just before December hit Michael got a call. It was Billy
Joel again. They were doing a month-long Millennium Tour
that would start December 1st. We called it the Y2K tour
since it ended on New Year's Eve in Madison Square Garden, New York City, 1999. What a way to ring in the century!
It was either going to be a big blast or a big bummer. There
was such uncertainty about how it would all go down. Some
predicted great computer failure, electrical storms, even a
chance of explosions- a perfect scenario for fear... the unknown. My dad likes to say F. E. A. R., false evidence ap-

pearing real. But for two God-fearing lovebirds this would be part of the adventure.

At least I knew Michael's schedule and could see when he would be in town and when he wouldn't. Michael was free to come home when there were more than two days between concerts. It really provided a tasteful bit of suspense without wearing me out. So not every day was a possibility. I was narrowing down the days. Hee hee!

December came in like a long awaited friend arriving on camel back from the Sahara Desert. Oh how I longed for this moment in my life. It had felt like forever. Now I was in it. I had terrific peace. I was trusting God and trusting Michael. How silly! I would be getting engaged. That was a given. It's amazing how we struggle with timing. Oh the humanity! Looking at his schedule I could see only a few possible options for this life-changing event. I imagined he might propose closer to Christmas. We would be around family. He would have a good paycheck by then. Hmm?

On December 14th I kissed him goodbye knowing I would see him on the 17th, as he had a couple of concerts back to back. One was in Indiana and the other a day later in Houston, Texas at what was formerly known as the Compact Center, now Lakewood Church. True story!

A dear friend of ours, Christine Stroupe, invited me out for dinner while Michael was away. She was a professional opera singer and needed to stop at the old Scarritt Bennett Chapel to pick up her Christmas music. I loved that old gothic stone building. I asked if I could go in with her. She smiled and said, "Sure!" It was loaded with character. When we stepped in the chapel I looked up and saw Michael sitting on the pipe organ bench. He was supposed to be on his way to Houston. It's the only time in my life that I almost passed out. Knowing what this meant completely blew me away.

He was all dressed up in a suit and had spread two-dozen Gerber daisies on the large stone communion table along with an old silver chalice of grape juice and French bread on a perfect little white plate. As he stepped down from the altar I could feel my knees get weak. It seemed like a dream. It was a dream. I just happened to be living it. His face was beaming. As he walked down the stairs he was laughing at how his plan had worked – I was laughing too and then crying and then laughing some more. Christine took our picture together and then bowed out.

This was a fine moment for Michael Mellett. After many hugs and kisses and the explanation that Billy had let him fly in for 24 hours, he took me by the hand to a grand piano and sang a song he had written called "Fiona, Will You Marry Me?" Each time we got to the chorus I looked at him as if to say, "Can I say *yes* yet?" He smiled, "Not yet."

After his song he got down on one knee and pulled that little black box from his jacket pocket. He gushed with words I never imagined hearing. There was no withholding. He laid his heart bare, unabashedly and with great delivery. I could hardly take in all the love and admiration of this amazingly brave heart. He was confident, composed, convinced, and unequivocally mine! I, in turn, was in awe, completely swept off my feet, overwhelmed at the privilege of this moment. I had never felt so esteemed in my whole life. It was as if a plethora of angels filled the chapel. The presence of God was tangible. This was not only Michael's moment, it was God's moment as well. Only he could have done this.

Michael led me to the altar to take communion. He wanted this to be the first thing we did as an engaged couple. He read a multitude of verses that expounded on God's love, his purposes, and his plan. We sat in awe of God, reflected on the details, and then practiced our walk down the aisle, taking it in, ever so slowly. This was not to be rushed.

I could feel God smiling. There was an awesome sense of purpose, kingdom, family, history, and faith. It all came together. This was not just an engagement. This was destiny! Michael had made reservations at Valentino's in downtown Nashville. He brought me home to get dressed up. I just happened to have a brand new, never worn, black dress with the tags still on. My mom had given it to me months previous. I didn't even know if it fit... But it did! And we were off to the restaurant. We called our families and reveled in the moment. Every second was precious.

The next day Michael made his way to Houston where Billy Joel announced our engagement as the "betrothed" from the platform of the Compact Center, now known as Lakewood Church. This was only the beginning. God was just warming up!

We traveled home together for Christmas and the Y2K concert, New Year's Eve in New York City. I'll never forget walking downtown Manhattan by the Twin Towers. It was a ghost town. It seemed like the only people headed into the city were those crazy enough to go to this concert. Michael was on the platform. I wondered how this would all work out. When we received our seats I realized Billy's daughter was sitting right in front of me and her bodyguard was right next to me. That felt pretty good! Of course nothing happened and it was all a bunch of hot air, but we sure did make a memory! And, the tour was quite a blessing in that it paid for my engagement ring! Thank you Jesus!

Engagement

Dating is one thing. Engagement is quite different. In Jewish culture it has the same weight as marriage in that it is taken very seriously. It's a unique time for a couple to ask important questions, go to pre-marital counseling, plan for life, write goals, and dream big. This too was not to be rushed. I didn't know how useful this time was until I was in the thick of it. This was not just about planning a wedding and how quickly it could be pulled off. It was about getting clarity on where we would be going in life, what kind of people we wanted to become and what kind of family we would raise. This took time.

I had pictured myself marrying a pastor or some famous evangelist. I was praying about what Latin American nation to go to next when God took me off-roading. There was no road to be seen, patches of dirt and lots of open land, but nothing was familiar. It would all be about trusting. The one thing I was completely convinced of was Michael. He was the man. Somehow, this would all come together. Michael loved people; he had a father's heart and a thriving life-group in his home. He pastored without the title. He loved the Spanish language and the people. He loved ministry and leading worship at Belmont Church; but, he was undoubtedly a vocal production man, sought after for his ability to create a beautiful backdrop for any major artist or group. He had a long history with the music industry and had worked hard to take his place in the community as a trusted vocal producer. His passion was in the studio and that was where he thrived. I learned to appreciate his gift; and, I embraced his life.

Once again Michael brought up the subject of letting go of my job. This time I could sense there was more to it for him. As the future head of the home he wanted to take a lead role in how we would work our finances and how we would trust God. The truth was that any vocal production opportunity paid far more that my regular job. He could see where we were headed. I had to let go and trust. It was a setup. Learning this early in our relationship was monumental. Yielding to God and a spouse is never about what you will lose, but about all you will gain. I could feel God was behind his words and I told him I would let go of it before we got married. Shortly after that conversation we started to receive more worship-recording work together. Michael could see a lot more than I could. He was right.

Pearl Power

It is very important to let the man lead in marriage. He will need some time to try out his skills and he will improve. The wife will need some growing room to create a loving and nurturing environment, to try out decorating and cooking abilities and to find a rhythm. She will improve too. Giving grace for these growing times is crucial to building trust instead of causing insecurities. Building a foundation starts during engagement when the waters are being tested in a sense. Words can be used to build one another up in a way that helps make these transitions smooth and keep things healthy. Find out your future spouse's love language, how they receive love best (*Five Love Languages* by Gary Smalley), and find out your own. It will take some of the guessing out of how to connect heart to heart.

The Wedding

We decided to get married in New York at the church I grew up in. The date was set for May 20, 2000. The pastor, Don Foster, was the same one who told me to call Michael five years previous. It all made a lot of sense now. The church was filled with over 400 guests. My father wore his

Irish kilt, as did the officiating pastor and some of Michael's relatives. We had an Uilleann bagpipe player filling the air with beautiful sounds, much like that of the movie Brave Heart. It was a perfectly misty Irish-looking day, which represented our heritage well. My relatives traveled from Ireland, many of our friends joined us from Nashville, and we were surrounded with long-time friends and family. Travis and Angela Cottrell led worship and the sanctuary was filled with joy and expectation. There was music for every moment. We were in no rush.

Since Michael had proposed with a song I surprised him during the ceremony and sang a song I wrote. As we led up to the vows, we took a moment to share what God had been speaking to our hearts. That morning while I was still in bed I sat up with my Bible and journal to talk to the Lord. I decided to go to 1 Corinthians, as it is known for themes of love, marriage, and relationships. As I read, there was a passage that jumped off the pages. I knew it was for us. It was certainly not your typical wedding passage, not even close, but I knew it was from God, for this day and I was to share it.

"For the foolishness of God is wiser than man's wisdom, and the weakness of God is stronger than man's strength. Brothers, think of what you were when you were called. Not many of you were wise by human standards; not many were influential; not many were of noble birth. But God chose the foolish things of the world to shame the wise; God chose the weak things of the world to shame the strong. He chose the lowly things of this world and the despised things- and the things that are not- to nullify the things that are, so that no one may boast before him. It is because of him that you are in Christ Jesus, who has become for us wisdom from

God- that is, our righteousness, holiness and redemption. Therefore, as it is written: Let him who
boasts boast in the Lord."—I Corinthians 1:25-31

As I shared the scripture, Michael shook his head in
amazement. He had that passage written on a piece of paper ready to read because it was exactly what God had given
him. It was settled, we could boast in the Lord because God
had done something marvelous with two people the world
might consider foolish, weak, non-influential, and of igno-
ble birth. God was making a point. He is not looking for the
smartest, most talented, most affluent, or most attractive
people. He's just looking for the most willing, no matter
what background you are from.

After the ceremony, we rode in a friend's 1963 Bentley
around Lake Mahopac, just as I had always dreamed. This
was one of my places to get alone with God, to learn to hear
his voice and follow his will. Now I was traveling the road
with my husband.

Following the reception, we headed to New York City
and then off to Donegal, Ireland, our "Irish Hawaii". There
was a deep peace and trust that filled our hearts from waiting for God's will and doing things his way. The only intimacy we knew was what we had between us and it was magnificent. Now we had a lifetime to grow, to give, and to nur-
ture. Waiting on God was more of a blessing than I could
have imagined. It made a lot more sense now that I was
married!

Pearl Power

Intimacy in marriage is awesome, precious, powerful, and holy. It's everything your heart hoped for and more. It cannot be duplicated in any other way. Hollywood cannot capture it because it is a secret. It is not for imaginations or for fantasy. It is for those who are willing to trust God and come into a covenant with him. It is sacred and absolutely worth the wait!

The Vision Fulfilled

Many things made more sense and took on greater meaning with marriage. Four days after we returned from our honeymoon in Ireland we boarded a plane once again, this time for Jerusalem. We were working for Integrity Music and our first international recording brought us to the Holy Land. What an honor! We also returned to Ireland that year. This time it was for a live worship recording. We sang in a cathedral with a big band and a full house. I thought to myself, "This must be basically the vision I had coming home from Billy Joel's birthday party." It wasn't exactly what I saw; but, what are the chances? I am in Ireland, with Michael Mellett, on a platform, with a band, leading worship. "Must be it," I thought.

Over the next few years we continued working on live recordings in Ireland, Singapore, Argentina, Costa Rica, Ecuador, and a myriad of domestic events. One conference we loved singing at was with Family Life. Within the first few years of our marriage we must have renewed our vows 25 times while doing these Rekindle the Romance conferences. On one occasion we sang at the Compact Center in Houston, Texas. This was where Billy Joel had announced our engagement. This time we heard that Lakewood Church, pastored by Joel Osteen, was in the process of acquiring the building. We were amazed by this church's faith and vision so we laid our hands on the walls and prayed that God would bless them, fill their seats, and bring everyone they would need to make this ministry flourish. It was only a few years later that we were asked to join their team as choir directors/music pastors. We gladly accepted.

Six months after our move to Texas, we joined a team ministering in England and Ireland. By this time Michael and I had been back to Ireland five times, but this trip was different. It was called a Night of Hope and it was being held in Belfast, very close to where my family is from. Many of my relatives came to the event. As usual, we assumed our positions on the platform in the middle of the band as the introductory music and video rolled. I'll never forget grabbing Michael's hand as the lights came up. It was the vision, exactly as I had seen it. Tears welled up as I leaned over to say, "This is it! This is what I saw!" Michael was amazed! It was an auditorium with white walls and a big blue curtain in the back, packed-out seats, a very full band, and precisely what I had witnessed that day we drove home from Billy Joel's house. I was in awe to say the least. It had been eight years since God revealed this moment to me. It affirmed everything we had pursued, letting us know we were undoubtedly in the center of God's will.

Pearl Power

God can give you a vision. You don't have to be an Old Testament prophet to have one. Joel 2:28 says, "And afterward, I will pour out my Spirit on all people. Your sons and daughters will prophesy, your old men will dream dreams, your young men will see visions." You can ask for God to speak to you through dreams and visions, to give you an idea of how to pray and believe for your destiny. When you sense God speaking to you, don't blow it off; write it down. Simple things can have such significance. Habakkuk 2:2 says, Write down the revelation (vision) and make it plain.... Though it linger, wait for it; it will certainly come and will not delay. When God speaks his truth to you, wait for it to come to pass. You will never regret waiting for God to fulfill his purposes in your life. Just ask!

God's Pearl Girl

Looking back now, **the most courageous thing I ever did was to follow Jesus.** I gave him the reins of my life. I asked for his will. It was not easy; but, there was always grace when I would yield my will to his. I didn't get it all perfect but I kept getting back to God. My brokenness became a tool. I found that people relate a whole lot better to real and broken than perfect and superficial. As I wrote this book, it wasn't until I had penned most of my journey as a single woman that I realized there was a theme running through my life. Pearls.

As a child I remember receiving my first real pearl necklace at a friend's wedding for being her flower girl. Once again, they adorned my neck the day of my sweet 16th birthday as well as my senior high school pictures and graduation day. Later, my father bought me the pearl ring in Ecuador as I had embraced my singleness and pursued God's calling on my life. In my Esther-moment, preparing for Billy Joel's birthday party, pearls were just the right thing to accompany this Michael Mellett. This time I bought them for myself. I even spoke to a band member at the party about how sometimes we are holding on so tightly to what is fake, like a fake string of pearls, when God wants to give us the real thing. On the day of my wedding, my father gave me away in an Italian designer wedding dress, drenched in pearls with pearl earrings, a pearl necklace, a pearl headpiece, and even shoes lined with rows of pearls. This time, it was all a gift from my parents.

As I was writing this book a dear friend gave me a pearl necklace for my birthday; and, for my anniversary, Michael gave me a fancy pearl bracelet with a heart locket on which he had inscribed on one side *Brave & Beautiful*, and on the other, *God's Pearl Girl*. One day as I held the bracelet in my hand I heard God say ever so clearly down deep in my spirit, "You ARE The Pearl!" I burst into tears because all along I had only thought of them as my adornment. I finally realized God had been calling me *the pearl* all this time.

In Matthew 13:45-46 it talks about the pearl of great price: "The kingdom of heaven is like a merchant looking for fine pearls. When he found one of great value, he went away and sold everything he had and bought it." We are precious, priceless pearls. Jesus gave up everything, including his throne to come to earth as a man and die for us in order to save us. He was this merchant looking for the pearl.

Scripture also says in Matthew 7:6, "Do not give dogs what is sacred; do not throw your pearls to pigs." God wants us to value ourselves, and value who we are in Him. He doesn't want us throwing ourselves out just anywhere for anything. God sees us as precious and priceless, something to give up everything for. As the great creator and designer of life, he knows us and understands us because he made us. He is the one who determines our worth. It takes some bravery to believe God at his word. The more we do, the more our beauty will blossom! No matter what you have been through or where you come from, *YOU* are God's Pearl! He calls *YOU* brave and beautiful! *And that's the truth*!

. . . .

A Prayer for You

Thank you Lord Jesus for the priceless Pearl that is reading this book. Please bless my dear friend with courage and strength to believe you, to trust you, and to surrender their whole life to you. Please teach my friend to pray and to seek you, to wait patiently for you. Help them to receive your grace every day in order to move forward. It is only in you that we find ourselves and live the abundant and extraordinary lives you have for us. In Jesus Mighty name!

. . . .

Today in Texas

Michael and I have five beautiful children who love Jesus: Colin Michael, Aiden Patrick, Celia Kate, Susana Grace (Gracie), and Sean Benjamin. This is my greatest ministry and my absolute treasure. I am so in love with my people!

Michael and I have the complete privilege of pastoring on staff at Lakewood Church, the largest church in the US. Michael directs and we co-pastor a choir of 400, as well as lead worship in the English and Spanish services with senior pastors Joel Osteen and Danilo Montero.

While I was still a single missionary, the Lord had given me a promise. One day as I read 1 Chronicles 17:25-26, the words jumped off the page. "You, my God, have revealed to your servant that you will build a house for him. So your servant has found courage to pray to you. O Lord, you are

God! You have promised these good things to your servant."
I sat up and said, "Lord! You're going to build me a house!"
It seemed quite literal. Mind you, I was living on $75 a
month and renting the maid's quarters, the smallest room I
ever had. There was absolutely no prospect of a house. I
didn't even have a husband, never mind finding a house!

Since being married to Michael we have always been
drawn to the country. We would take drives through Nashville each Saturday to get to the country as we dreamed of
the day we would live there. When we moved to Texas we
did the same thing. Every Saturday was a good day to look
for horses, longhorns, country markets, antique shops, and
anything else that piqued our interest out in the country.

After 12 years of hoping, waiting and praying, we
moved into our dream home out in the country. As we
packed up, I was reminded of the promise God had given
me as a single missionary. We found out that they had
built the house in 1992. My Bible, which I've used since I
was 18, has that specific scripture marked "early '90s." God
wasn't kidding! He never is! Today I have the best job in
the world, loving on my beautiful family of 7. I can't wait
to tell you the rest. God has done exceedingly abundantly
more than I could have asked. The miracles keep coming.
And so the story continues...

We Care About Your Life and Your Future

In every heart there is a God-shaped hole that only He can fill. We may try other things to find love, peace and joy but developing a relationship with our Heavenly Father through his son, Jesus Christ is where real life begins. God wanted a family and that is why he created you. He wants to help you, guide you, fill you with peace and give you hope and a future, all because he loves you.

You can start this relationship today by praying, "Jesus, I reach my heart out to yours. I believe you died for me and rose from the dead. I want to live my life following you. I turn away from my sins and ask that you would forgive me. Today I place my trust in you. Please give me a clean, fresh start. You are my Savior and Lord. Please guide my life from now on."

It's that simple. This is the beginning of establishing a close relationship with God. Now you can help yourself grow by reading the Bible and talking to God through prayer. Reading a portion of Psalms, Proverbs, and the New Testament is a great way to start. You may also want to write in a journal to express your heart to him or to write questions that you can ask a pastor. Finding a good Bible-based church will help you grow as you are surrounded by other people of faith and will have a pastor you can talk to. But remember, God can talk to you anywhere and you can ask him to explain the Bible to you by his Holy Spirit. He said he will "never leave you or forsake you". He is so faithful. Give yourself some grace as you are in this process. You won't get it all right. The Bible says, "A righteous man may fall seven times but he gets right back up." You are not righteous because you don't fall. You are righteous because of Jesus. Get back up and keep running to him. And you will find he is the truest, kindest, and most loving Father. He loves you so very much!

Stay In Touch

Michael and I would love to hear from you.
Feel free to write us at...

www.FionaMellett.com
www.BeBraveandBeautiful.com
www.M7ministries.com

Follow us on Facebook and Twitter:

Facebook.com/BraveandBeautiful.FionaMellett
Twitter.com/@BraveBeautiful1
Facebook.com/FionaMellett
Twitter.com/@Fiona_Mellett